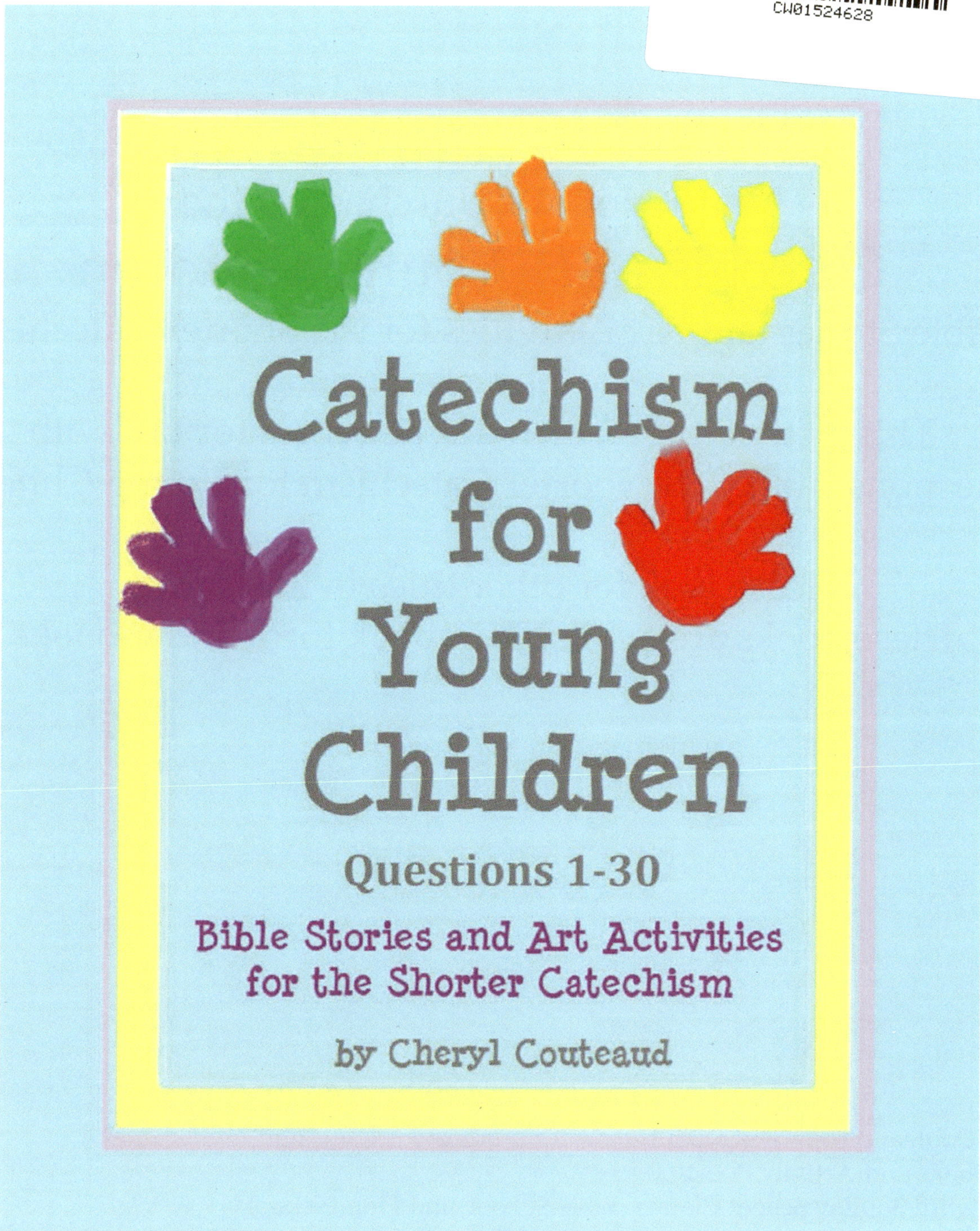

Catechism for Young Children

Questions 1-30

Bible Stories and Art Activities for the Shorter Catechism

by Cheryl Couteaud

Catechism for Young Children
Bible Stories and Art Activities for Use with the Shorter Catechism
©2013 Cheryl Couteaud

Thank you for purchasing the
Catechism for Young Children
Bible Stories and Art Activities for the Shorter Catechism

This Activity Book contains activities for use with
Questions 1-30 of the Shorter Catechism for Young Children

Please look for other titles in this series.
These books are available in book form and e-books.

Cheryl Couteaud copyright ©2013
Color Books and Activity Books
For use with Sunday School Classes, Bible School, and Homeschool
Look for other titles available in soft cover and e-book formats.

*Scripture taken from the Holy Bible, NEW INTERNATIONAL VERSION. Copyright © 1973, 1978, 1984, International Bible Society. Used by permission of Zondervan Bible Publishers. (Unless otherwise noted.)

1. Question: *Who made you?*
Answer: **God!**

> **Bible Reference:**
> For You created my inmost being; You knit me together in my mother's womb. I praise you for I am fearfully and wonderfully made; your works are wonderful, I know that full well.
> *Psalm 139: 13 & 14*

Art Activity:

choice one

Our bodies:
"God made ME!"

Materials:
- Butcher paper
- Permanent marker
- Washable markers or paint
- Scissors and tape

....

Roll out butcher paper. Have child lie on paper and trace around his/her body with permanent marker. Cut out and tape body to floor. Let child color with markers or paint.

choice two

Our handprints.
"God made ME!"

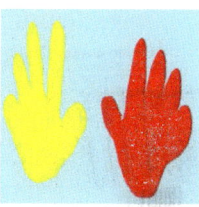

Materials:
- Heavy paper
- Watercolor or washable tempera paint
- Paint brush
- Wet wash cloth or baby wipes to clean hands with

....

Paint each child's hands with paint. Press hands on to paper and lift off. Write, "God made me," on the paper!

Genesis 1

The Beginning

1 In the beginning God created the heavens and the earth. 2 Now the earth was formless and empty, darkness was over the surface of the deep, and the Spirit of God was hovering over the waters. 3 And God said, "Let there be light," and there was light. 4 God saw that the light was good, and he separated the light from the darkness. 5 God called the light "day," and the darkness he called "night." And there was evening, and there was morning—the first day. 6 And God said, "Let there be a vault between the waters to separate water from water." 7 So God made the vault and separated the water under the vault from the water above it. And it was so. 8 God called the vault "sky." And there was evening, and there was morning—the second day. 9 And God said, "Let the water under the sky be gathered to one place, and let dry ground appear." And it was so. 10 God called the dry ground "land," and the gathered waters he called "seas." And God saw that it was good. 11 Then God said, "Let the land produce vegetation: seed-bearing plants and trees on the land that bear fruit with seed in it, according to their various kinds." And it was so. 12 The land produced vegetation: plants bearing seed according to their kinds and trees bearing fruit with seed in it according to their kinds. And God saw that it was good. 13 And there was evening, and there was morning—the third day. 14 And God said, "Let there be lights in the vault of the sky to separate the day from the night, and let them serve as signs to mark sacred times, and days and years, 15 and let them be lights in the vault of the sky to give light on the earth." And it was so. 16 God made two great lights—the greater light to govern the day and the lesser light to govern the night. He also made the stars. 17 God set them in the vault of the sky to give light on the earth, 18 to govern the day and the night, and to separate light from darkness. And God saw that it was good. 19 And there was evening, and there was morning—the fourth day. 20 And God said, "Let the water teem with living creatures, and let birds fly above the earth across the vault of the sky." 21 So God created the great creatures of the sea and every living thing with which the water teems and that moves about in it, according to their kinds, and every winged bird according to its kind. And God saw that it was good. 22 God blessed them and said, "Be fruitful and increase in number and fill the water in the seas, and let the birds increase on the earth." 23 And there was evening, and there was morning—the fifth day. 24 And God said, "Let the land produce living creatures according to their kinds: the livestock, the creatures that move along the ground, and the wild animals, each according to its kind." And it was so. 25 God made the wild animals according to their kinds, the livestock according to their kinds, and all the creatures that move along the ground according to their kinds. And God saw that it was good. 26 Then God said, "Let us make mankind in our image, in our likeness, so that they may rule over the fish in the sea and the birds in the sky, over the livestock and all the wild animals, and over all the creatures that move along the ground."

27 So God created mankind in his own image, in the image of God he created them; male and female he created them. 28 God blessed them and said to them, "Be fruitful and increase in number; fill the earth and subdue it. Rule over the fish in the sea and the birds in the sky and over every living creature that moves on the ground." 29 Then God said, "I give you every seed-bearing plant on the face of the whole earth and every tree that has fruit with seed in it. They will be yours for food. 30 And to all the beasts of the earth and all the birds in the sky and all the creatures that move along the ground—everything that has the breath of life in it—I give every green plant for food." And it was so. 31 God saw all that he had made, and it was very good. And there was evening, and there was morning—the sixth day.

New International Version (NIV)

2. Question: *What else did God make?*

Answer: **God made all things!**

> Bible Reference: Genesis One!   (Read aloud in class or use Creation coloring book.)

Art Activity:

choice one

Creation Collage:

Materials:

- Magazine cutouts
- Construction paper
- Glue
- Marker

....

Have magazine pictures already cut out before coming to class and write title on paper beforehand as well. Children glue pictures of things God created onto paper.

choice two

Creation Picture:

Materials:

- Heavy paper
- Paint and paint brushes
- Paper towels or wipes
- Water in sandwich meat tubs

....

Write title on paper with permanent marker. Let children paint (or draw) a picture of something God made.

The Ten Commandments

20 And God spoke all these words:

² "I am the LORD your God, who brought you out of Egypt, out of the land of slavery.

³ "You shall have no other gods before[a] me.

⁴ "You shall not make for yourself an image in the form of anything in heaven above or on the earth beneath or in the waters below. ⁵ You shall not bow down to them or worship them; for I, the LORD your God, am a jealous God, punishing the children for the sin of the parents to the third and fourth generation of those who hate me, ⁶ but showing love to a thousand generations of those who love me and keep my commandments.

⁷ "You shall not misuse the name of the LORD your God, for the LORD will not hold anyone guiltless who misuses his name.

⁸ "Remember the Sabbath day by keeping it holy. ⁹ Six days you shall labor and do all your work, ¹⁰ but the seventh day is a sabbath to the LORD your God. On it you shall not do any work, neither you, nor your son or daughter, nor your male or female servant, nor your animals, nor any foreigner residing in your towns. ¹¹ For in six days the LORD made the heavens and the earth, the sea, and all that is in them, but he rested on the seventh day. Therefore the LORD blessed the Sabbath day and made it holy.

¹² "Honor your father and your mother, so that you may live long in the land the LORD your God is giving you.

¹³ "You shall not murder.

¹⁴ "You shall not commit adultery.

¹⁵ "You shall not steal.

¹⁶ "You shall not give false testimony against your neighbor.

¹⁷ "You shall not covet your neighbor's house. You shall not covet your neighbor's wife, or his male or female servant, his ox or donkey, or anything that belongs to your neighbor."

3. Question: *Why did God make you and all things?*
Answer: **For his own glory!**

4. Question: *How can you glorify God?*
Answer: By loving Him and doing what he commands!

Bible Reference: 1st Corinthians 13 and The Ten Commandments Exodus 20: 1-17
(Read aloud in class)

1st Corinthians 13

13 If I speak in the tongues[a] of men or of angels, but do not have love, I am only a resounding gong or a clanging cymbal. 2 If I have the gift of prophecy and can fathom all mysteries and all knowledge, and if I have a faith that can move mountains, but do not have love, I am nothing. 3 If I give all I possess to the poor and give over my body to hardship that I may boast,[b] but do not have love, I gain nothing.

4 Love is patient, love is kind. It does not envy, it does not boast, it is not proud. 5 It does not dishonor others, it is not self-seeking, it is not easily angered, it keeps no record of wrongs. 6 Love does not delight in evil but rejoices with the truth. 7 It always protects, always trusts, always hopes, always perseveres.

8 Love never fails. But where there are prophecies, they will cease; where there are tongues, they will be stilled; where there is knowledge, it will pass away. 9 For we know in part and we prophesy in part, 10 but when completeness comes, what is in part disappears. 11 When I was a child, I talked like a child, I thought like a child, I reasoned like a child. When I became a man, I put the ways of childhood behind me. 12 For now we see only a reflection as in a mirror; then we shall see face to face. Now I know in part; then I shall know fully, even as I am fully known.

13 And now these three remain: faith, hope and love. But the greatest of these is love.

Art Activity
<u>choice one</u>

Valentines For God

Materials:
- Tissue paper
- Construction paper
- Glue and scissors

Glue torn pieces of tissue paper to Heart shaped pieces of construction Paper. Write: The Greatest of these is love!

Role Play
<u>choice two</u>

Have children act out doing what God commands.

- **Sharing Toys**
- **Loving one another**
- **Obeying Mom or Dad**
  - brushing your teeth, cleaning up, going to bed, eating dinner, being nice to siblings, etc.

Psalm 23

The Lord is My Shepherd

Psalm 23

King James Version (KJV)

23 The LORD is my shepherd; I shall not want.

² He maketh me to lie down in green pastures: he leadeth me beside the still waters.

³ He restoreth my soul: he leadeth me in the paths of righteousness for his name's sake.

⁴ Yea, though I walk through the valley of the shadow of death, I will fear no evil: for thou art with me; thy rod and thy staff they comfort me.

⁵ Thou preparest a table before me in the presence of mine enemies: thou anointest my head with oil; my cup runneth over.

⁶ Surely goodness and mercy shall follow me all the days of my life: and I will dwell in the house of the LORD forever.

5. Question: *Why ought you to glorify God?*

Answer: **Because he made me and takes care of me!**

Bible Reference Luke 12: 22-31 and Psalm 23

[22] Then Jesus said to his disciples: "Therefore I tell you, do not worry about your life, what you will eat; or about your body, what you will wear. [23] For life is more than food, and the body more than clothes. [24] Consider the ravens: They do not sow or reap, they have no storeroom or barn; yet God feeds them. And how much more valuable you are than birds! [25] Who of you by worrying can add a single hour to your life [26] Since you cannot do this very little thing, why do you worry about the rest?

[27] "Consider the lilies how they grow. They do not labor or spin. Yet I tell you, not even Solomon in all his splendor was dressed like one of these. [28] If that is how God clothes the grass of the field, which is here today, and tomorrow is thrown into the fire, how much more will he clothe you—you of little faith! [29] And do not set your heart on what you will eat or drink; do not worry about it. [30] For the pagan world runs after all such things, and your Father knows that you need them. [31] But seek his kingdom, and these things will be given to you as well.   **Luke 12: 22-31**

Art Activity:
"Needs Mobile"

Materials:
- Yarn
- Scissors
- Stick or dowel or metal coat hanger
- Precut pictures of needs (Can be made from anything from magazine pictures to photos to pieces of fabric or little plastic toys)
- Hole puncher

(A second art option is making tissue paper lilies… for symbolism. Glue tissue paper to colored construction paper in the shape of lilies.)

6. Question: *Are there more Gods than one?*

Answer: **There is only one God!**

7. Question: *In how many persons does this one God exist?*

Answer: In three persons

8. Question: **What are they?**

Answer: *The Father, the Son, and the Holy Ghost*

Bible Reference: Matthew 3:13-17 (The Baptism of Jesus) Father, Son, and Holy Ghost
Matthew 3:13-17 (New International Version)

[13] Then Jesus came from Galilee to the Jordan to be baptized by John. [14] But John tried to deter him, saying, "I need to be baptized by you, and do you come to me?" [15] Jesus replied, "Let it be so now; it is proper for us to do this to fulfill all righteousness." Then John consented. [16] As soon as Jesus was baptized, he went up out of the water. At that moment heaven was opened, and he saw the Spirit of God descending like a dove and alighting on him. [17] And a voice from heaven said, "This is my Son, whom I love; with him I am well pleased."

Art Activity:
A Dove   or the Trinity

Materials:
- Precut dove shape
- Glue
- Feathers

Cut out the shape of a dove and glue feathers to it.

Materials:
- Stickers or precut shapes of symbols for the Trinity (cross, dove, light)
- Precut triangles from Construction Paper

Glue or place stickers or pictures to the Triangle in the corners.

9. Question: *What is God?*

Answer: **God is a Spirit and has not a body like men!**

10. Question: *Where is God?*

Answer: God is everywhere!

11. Question: *Can you see God?*

Answer: No, I cannot see God, but he always sees me.

> Bible Reference: John 3: 8 "The wind blows wherever it pleases. You hear its sound, but you cannot tell where it comes from or where it is going. So it is with everyone born of the Spirit."

Art Activity:

A leaf on a string blowing in the wind.
You cannot see the wind, but you can see what the wind does…. Just like the Holy Spirit. Just like God.

Materials:
- **Construction paper**
- **Tissue paper**
- **Glue**
- **Hole puncher**
- **String or yarn**

Cut a leaf shape from the construction paper. Cut the middle out as well. Glue tissue paper across the opening. Punch a hole in the stem and tie a piece of string to it.

12. Question: *Does God Know all things?*

Answer: **Yes, nothing can be hidden from God.**

13. Question: *Can God do all things?*

Answer: Yes, God can do all his Holy will!

Art Activity:
Picture of things God made:

Materials:
- Drawing paper
- Crayons or markers

Have children draw a picture of something God has done.

Bible Reference: Psalm 139: 1-10

You have searched me, LORD,
 and you know me.
² You know when I sit and when I rise;
 you perceive my thoughts from afar.
³ You discern my going out and my lying down;
 you are familiar with all my ways.
⁴ Before a word is on my tongue
 you, LORD, know it completely.
⁵ You hem me in behind and before,
 and you lay your hand upon me.
⁶ Such knowledge is too wonderful for me,
 too lofty for me to attain.

⁷ Where can I go from your Spirit?
 Where can I flee from your presence?
⁸ If I go up to the heavens, you are there;
 if I make my bed in the depths, you are there.
⁹ If I rise on the wings of the dawn,
 if I settle on the far side of the sea,
¹⁰ even there your hand will guide me,
 your right hand will hold me fast.

14. Question: *Where do you learn how to love and obey God?*

Answer: **In the Bible alone.**

15. Question: *Who wrote the Bible?*

Answer: Holy men who were taught by the Holy Spirit.

Bible Reference: Revelation 22: 18&19

[18] I warn everyone who hears the words of the prophecy of this scroll: If anyone adds anything to them, God will add to that person the plagues described in this scroll. [19] And if anyone takes words away from this scroll of prophecy, God will take away from that person any share in the tree of life and in the Holy City, which are described in this scroll.

Art Activity:
Bible Scroll

Materials:
- Two dowels
- Markers
- Long, thin paper

Write Psalm 119:11 on scrolls or use the books of the Bible. Have children draw a picture or illustrate their scrolls.

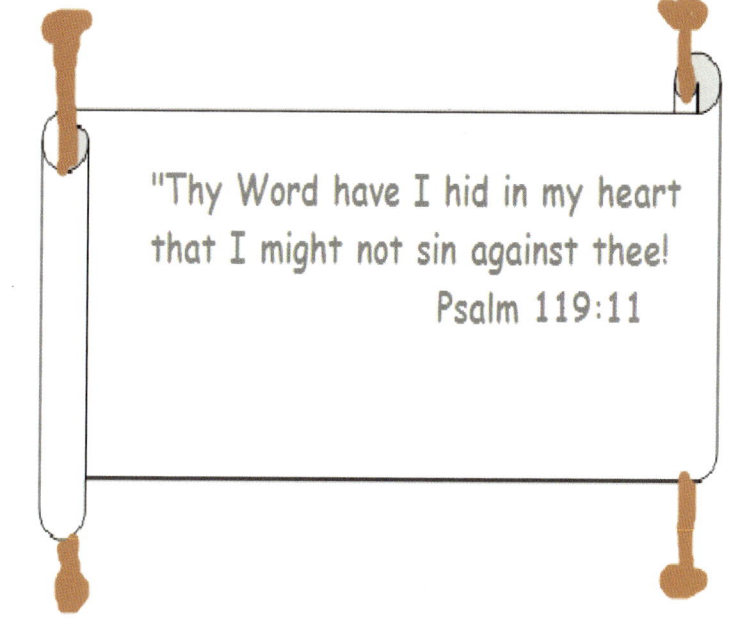

16. Question: *Who were our first parents?*

Answer: **Adam and Eve**

> **Bible Reference: Genesis 3:20**
> ²⁰ "Adam named his wife Eve, because she would become the mother of all the living."

Art Activity:
Baby Collage

Materials:
- Precut pictures of babies from magazines
- Glue
- Construction paper

Glue pictures of all the babies onto construction paper. This could also be done on one big banner for the wall. (Another idea is to draw a picture of the world in the middle of the page or banner.)

17. Question: *Of what were out first parents made?*

Answer: God made the body of Adam out of the ground and formed Eve from the body of Adam

18. Question: *What did God give Adam and Eve besides bodies?*

Answer: He gave them souls that could never die.

> **Bible Reference: Genesis 2:20-24 (NIV)**
>
> [20] So the man gave names to all the livestock, the birds in the sky and all the wild animals.
>
> But for Adam no suitable helper was found. [21] So the LORD God caused the man to fall into a deep sleep; and while he was sleeping, he took one of the man's ribs and then closed up the place with flesh. [22] Then the LORD God made a woman from the rib he had taken out of the man, and he brought her to the man.
>
> [23] The man said,
>
> "This is now bone of my bones
>   and flesh of my flesh;
> she shall be called 'woman,'
>   for she was taken out of man."
>
> [24] That is why a man leaves his father and mother and is united to his wife, and they become one flesh.

Art Activity:
Sculpture

Materials:

- Party size play dough

Instruct students to make Adam from their play dough. Have Adam "fall into a deep sleep" and take one of his ribs (a pinch of play dough) and form Eve out of it by adding more play dough.

Have students try to make the figures come alive… "Only God can give life…and a soul…."

19. Question: *Have you a soul as well as a body?*

Answer: Yes, I have a soul that can never die.

20. Question: *How do you know that you have a soul?*

Answer: Because the Bible tells me so.

Bible References:
Genesis 1:26-27
Romans 1:19-20
Psalm 62:1

Art Activity:
The Bible

Materials:

- White construction paper
- Black construction paper torn into pieces
- Glue
- Glitter
- Catechism questions and answers numbers 19 and 20 printed for each student

Glue torn pieces of black paper to back of white paper. Fold in half so that the black is on the outside. Write "Holy Bible" on front with glue and then sprinkle glitter on it so that the letters are in gold. Glue question to the inside of the "Bible."

²⁶ Then God said, "Let us make mankind in our image, in our likeness, so that they may rule over the fish in the sea and the birds in the sky, over the livestock and all the wild animals, and over all the creatures that move along the ground."

²⁷ So God created mankind in his own image, in the image of God he created them;
    male and female he created them.

Genesis 1:26-27

¹⁹ Since what may be known about God is plain to them, because God has made it plain to them. ²⁰ For since the creation of the world God's invisible qualities—his eternal power and divine nature—have been clearly seen, being understood from what has been made, so that people are without excuse.

Romans 1:19-20

Psalm 62:1
Truly my **soul** finds rest in God; my salvation comes from him.

21. Question: In what condition did God make Adam and Eve?
Answer: He made them Holy and Happy!

Bible References: Genesis 1 & 2 (See page 4 for Genesis 1) [4] This is the account of the heavens and the earth when they were created, when the LORD God made the earth and the heavens.

[5] Now no shrub had yet appeared on the earth and no plant had yet sprung up, for the LORD God had not sent rain on the earth and there was no one to work the ground, [6] but streams came up from the earth and watered the whole surface of the ground. [7] Then the LORD God formed a man from the dust of the ground and breathed into his nostrils the breath of life, and the man became a living being.

[8] Now the LORD God had planted a garden in the east, in Eden; and there he put the man he had formed. [9] The LORD God made all kinds of trees grow out of the ground—trees that were pleasing to the eye and good for food. In the middle of the garden were the tree of life and the tree of the knowledge of good and evil.

[10] A river watering the garden flowed from Eden; from there it was separated into four headwaters. [11] The name of the first is the Pishon; it winds through the entire land of Havilah, where there is gold. [12] (The gold of that land is good; aromatic resinand onyx are also there.) [13] The name of the second river is the Gihon; it winds through the entire land of Cush. [14] The name of the third river is the Tigris; it runs along the east side of Ashur. And the fourth river is the Euphrates.

Art Activity:
Adam and Eve Puppets

Materials:

- Small paper plates
- Popsicle sticks
- Yarn for hair
- Wiggle eyes
- Markers or construction paper
- Hole puncher

Cut out flesh colored pieces of construction paper is circles to go to paper plates or have students color plates with markers or crayons (or paint.) Glue on wiggle eyes and draw a mouth and a nose. Punch holes into the top of the plates with a whole puncher and tie yarn through holes for hair. Glue a Popsicle stick to the bottom for a handle. Write child's name onto the back of his puppets. Either make two puppets for each child, one Adam and the other Eve or make a two faced puppet with Adam on one side and Eve on the other…

22. Question: What is a covenant?
Answer: An agreement between two or more persons.

23. Question: What covenant did God make with Adam?
Answer: The Covenant of works.

24. Question: What was Adam bound to do by the Covenant of Works?
Answer: To obey God perfectly.

> **Bible References:**
> Genesis 2:15-17 ¹⁵ The LORD God took the man and put him in the Garden of Eden to work it and take care of it. ¹⁶ And the LORD God commanded the man, "You are free to eat from any tree in the garden; ¹⁷ but you must not eat from the tree of the knowledge of good and evil, for when you eat from it you will certainly die."

Art Activity:
The Tree of the knowledge of Good and Evil

Materials:

- Torn pieces of construction paper- green and brown
- A blue piece of construction paper
- Glue
- Type questions and verses and Glue them to the back

25. Question: *What did God promise in the Covenant of Works?*
Answer: To reward Adam with Life if Adam obeyed Him.

26. Question: *What did God threaten in the Covenant of Works?*
Answer: God threatened to punish Adam with death if Adam disobeyed Him.

> **Bible References:**
> **Genesis Genesis 2:9**
> ⁹ The LORD God made all kinds of trees grow out of the ground—trees that were pleasing to the eye and good for food. In the middle of the garden were the tree of life and the tree of the knowledge of good and evil.
> **Genesis 2:16&17,** ¹⁶ And the LORD God commanded the man, "You are free to eat from any tree in the garden; ¹⁷ but you must not eat from the tree of the knowledge of good and evil, for when you eat from it you will certainly die."
> **Genesis 3:22-24** ²² And the LORD God said, "The man has now become like one of us, knowing good and evil. He must not be allowed to reach out his hand and take also from the tree of life and eat, and live forever." ²³ So the LORD God banished him from the Garden of Eden to work the ground from which he had been taken. ²⁴ After he drove the man out, he placed on the east side[e] of the Garden of Eden cherubim and a flaming sword flashing back and forth to guard the way to the tree of life.

Art Activity:
The Tree of the knowledge of Life!

Materials: *(It is important to do each tree so that children know of both.)*

- Torn pieces of tissue paper- green and brown
- Blue pieces of construction paper
- Glue
- Type questions and verses and glue them to the back

Genesis 3 The Fall

New International Version (NIV)

3 Now the serpent was more crafty than any of the wild animals the LORD God had made. He said to the woman, "Did God really say, 'You must not eat from any tree in the garden'?"

² The woman said to the serpent, "We may eat fruit from the trees in the garden, ³ but God did say, 'You must not eat fruit from the tree that is in the middle of the garden, and you must not touch it, or you will die.'"

⁴ "You will not certainly die," the serpent said to the woman. ⁵ "For God knows that when you eat from it your eyes will be opened, and you will be like God, knowing good and evil."

⁶ When the woman saw that the fruit of the tree was good for food and pleasing to the eye, and also desirable for gaining wisdom, she took some and ate it. She also gave some to her husband, who was with her, and he ate it. ⁷ Then the eyes of both of them were opened, and they realized they were naked; so they sewed fig leaves together and made coverings for themselves. ⁸ Then the man and his wife heard the sound of the LORD God as he was walking in the garden in the cool of the day, and they hid from the LORD God among the trees of the garden.

⁹ But the LORD God called to the man, "Where are you?"

¹⁰ He answered, "I heard you in the garden, and I was afraid because I was naked; so I hid."

¹¹ And he said, "Who told you that you were naked? Have you eaten from the tree that I commanded you not to eat from?"

¹² The man said, "The woman you put here with me—she gave me some fruit from the tree, and I ate it."

¹³ Then the LORD God said to the woman, "What is this you have done?

"The woman said, "The serpent deceived me, and I ate."¹⁴ So the LORD God said to the serpent, "Because you have done this, "Cursed are you above all livestock and all wild animals! You will crawl on your belly and you will eat dust all the days of your life. ¹⁵ And I will put enmity between you and the woman, and between your offspring and hers; he will crush your head, and you will strike his heel."¹⁶

To the woman he said, "I will make your pains in childbearing very severe; with painful labor you will give birth to children.
Your desire will be for your husband, and he will rule over you."

¹⁷ To Adam he said, "Because you listened to your wife and ate fruit from the tree about which I commanded you, 'You must not eat from it,' "Cursed is the ground because of you; through painful toil you will eat food from it all the days of your life. ¹⁸ It will produce thorns and thistles for you, and you will eat the plants of the field. ¹⁹ By the sweat of your brow you will eat your food until you return to the ground, since from it you were taken; for dust you are and to dust you will return."

²⁰ Adam named his wife Eve, because she would become the mother of all the living.²¹ The LORD God made garments of skin for Adam and his wife and clothed them. ²² And the LORD God said, "The man has now become like one of us, knowing good and evil. He must not be allowed to reach out his hand and take also from the tree of life and eat, and live forever." ²³ So the LORD God banished him from the Garden of Eden to work the ground from which he had been taken. ²⁴ After he drove the man out, he placed on the east side of the Garden of Eden cherubim and a flaming sword flashing back and forth to guard the way to the tree of life.

27. Question: Did Adam keep the Covenant of Works?
Answer: No, He sinned against God.

Bible References:
Genesis 3

Art Activity:

Choice One
A Forbidden Fruit

Materials:
- Styrofoam ball
- Glue
- Pipe Cleaner
- Tissue paper

Glue tissue paper to Styrofoam shape. Insert Pipe Cleaner into top and form into a leaf shape. Cover the leaf Shape with tissue paper- making a tissue paper leaf.

Choice Two
A Snake

Materials:
- Paint or Tissue Paper
- Brushes or Glue
- Construction Paper

Have children paint a snake or glue pieces of torn tissue paper onto a sheet of construction paper. Make sure you add a forked tongue. Cut snake out so that it is more life like.

28. Question: What is a Sin?

Answer. Any thought, word, or deed that breaks God's law by omission or commission.

29. Question: What is a sin of omission?

Answer: Not being or doing what God requires.

30. Question: What is a sin of commission?

Answer: Doing what God forbids.

> Bible References:
> James 4:17
> [17] If anyone, then, knows the good they ought to do and doesn't do it, it is sin for them.
> 1 John 3:4
> [4] Everyone who sins breaks the law; in fact, sin is lawlessness.

Art Activity:
Sin Collection

Materials:

- Large black poster board to hang on the wall
- Pieces of torn construction paper of all colors (@ 3"x4")
- Black markers

Hang poster board on the wall and pass out torn pieces of construction paper. Have children write all kinds of "sins" onto their pieces of construction paper and take turns hanging them on the poster board. Say, "Sins come in all shapes and colors…"

Thank you for purchasing the
Catechism for Young Children
Bible Stories and Art Activities for the Shorter Catechism

This Activity Book contains activities to do with Questions 1-30

Please look for other titles in the series.
These books are available in book form and e-books.

copyright©2013 Cheryl Couteaud

*Scripture taken from the Holy Bible, NEW INTERNATIONAL VERSION. Copyright © 1973, 1978, 1984, International Bible Society. Used by permission of Zondervan Bible Publishers.

Printed in Great Britain
by Amazon.co.uk, Ltd.,
Marston Gate.

TABLE OF CONTENT

CHAPTER 1 11

UNDERSTANDING ADHD 11

   History of ADHD Diet 11

   The Role of Nutrition in Managing ADHD Symptoms 12

   5 Benefits of an ADHD Diet 13

   Practical Tips for Implementing an ADHD Diet 13

CHAPTER 2 15

BREAKFAST RECIPES 15

   Avocado and Egg Toast 15

   Banana and Almond Butter Smoothie 16

   Greek Yogurt Parfait 17

   Sweet Potato and Spinach Hash 18

   Quinoa Breakfast Bowl 19

   Veggie Omelette with Goat Cheese 20

   Chickpea Pancakes with Spinach and Tomato 21

   Baked Sweet Potato and Black Bean Hash ... 22

   Smoked Salmon and Avocado Wrap 23

   Apple Cinnamon Quinoa Porridge 24

CHAPTER 3 26

LUNCH RECIPES 26

   Grilled Chicken and Quinoa Salad 26

   Lentil and Vegetable Stir-Fry 27

   Turkey and Avocado Lettuce Wraps 28

   Salmon and Quinoa Stuffed Peppers 30

   Chickpea and Spinach Salad 31

   Lentil and Vegetable Soup 32

   Butternut Squash and Black Bean Tacos 33

   Quinoa and Edamame Salad 34

   Grilled Portobello Mushroom and Quinoa Bowl 36

   Zucchini Noodles with Pesto and Grilled Shrimp 37

CHAPTER 4 38

SNACKS AND DIPS 38

   Carrot Sticks with Tahini Dip 38

   Cucumber Slices with Avocado Dip 39

   Celery Sticks with Almond Butter Dip 40

   Bell Pepper Strips with Hummus 41

   Apple Slices with Sunflower Seed Butter Dip 42

   Jicama Sticks with Guacamole 43

   Radish Slices with Beet Hummus 44

   Sweet Potato Chips with Avocado Dip 45

   Zucchini Chips with Greek Yogurt Dill Dip 46

Cucumber Rounds with Spicy Chickpea Dip 47

CHAPTER 5 49

SOUP AND STEW 49

    Lentil and Spinach Soup 49

    Butternut Squash and Chickpea Stew 50

    Carrot Ginger Soup 52

    Moroccan Lentil Stew 53

    Sweet Potato and Red Lentil Soup 54

    Chickpea and Kale Stew 56

    Green Pea and Mint Soup 57

    Eggplant and Tomato Stew 58

    Broccoli and Cauliflower Soup 59

    White Bean and Kale Stew 61

CHAPTER 6 62

DINNER RECIPES 62

    Quinoa-Stuffed Bell Peppers 62

    Baked Salmon with Asparagus and Sweet Potato 64

    Stuffed Portobello Mushrooms 65

    Grilled Chicken with Quinoa and Roasted Vegetables 66

    Baked Cod with Herb Quinoa and Steamed Broccoli 68

    Turkey and Vegetable Stir-Fry 69

Grilled Shrimp with Avocado and Mango Salad 70

Lentil and Spinach Curry 71

Grilled Eggplant with Chickpea and Tomato Salad 73

Turkey Meatballs with Zucchini Noodles 74

CHAPTER 7 75

30 DAYS MEAL PLAN 75

Week 1 75

    Day 1 75

        Breakfast 75

        Lunch 75

        Snack 75

        Soup 75

        Dinner 75

    Day 2 75

        Breakfast 75

        Lunch 75

        Snack 75

        Stew 75

        Dinner 75

    Day 3 76

        Breakfast 76

        Lunch 76

        Snack 76

Soup	76
Dinner	76
Day 4	**76**
Breakfast	76
Lunch	76
Snack	76
Stew	76
Dinner	76
Day 5	**76**
Breakfast	76
Lunch	76
Snack	76
Soup	76
Dinner	76
Day 6	**76**
Breakfast	76
Lunch	76
Snack	76
Stew	76
Dinner	76
Day 7	**76**
Breakfast	76
Lunch	76
Snack	76
Soup	76
Dinner	76
Week 2	**77**
Day 8	**77**
Breakfast	77
Lunch	77
Snack	77
Stew	77
Dinner	77
Day 9	**77**
Breakfast	77
Lunch	77
Snack	77
Soup	77
Dinner	77
Day 10	**78**
Breakfast	78
Lunch	78
Snack	78
Stew	78
Dinner	78
Day 11	**78**
Breakfast	78
Lunch	78

Snack	78	Lunch	79
Soup	78	Snack	79
Dinner	78	Soup	79
Day 12	78	Dinner	79
Breakfast	78	Day 16	79
Lunch	78	Breakfast	79
Snack	78	Lunch	79
Stew	78	Snack	79
Dinner	78	Stew	79
Day 13	78	Dinner	79
Breakfast	78	Day 17	79
Lunch	78	Breakfast	79
Snack	78	Lunch	79
Soup	78	Snack	79
Dinner	78	Soup	79
Day 14	78	Dinner	79
Breakfast	78	Day 18	79
Lunch	78	Breakfast	79
Snack	78	Lunch	79
Stew	78	Snack	79
Dinner	78	Stew	79
Week 3	79	Dinner	79
Day 15	79	Day 19	79
Breakfast	79	Breakfast	79

Lunch 79	Breakfast 80
Snack 80	Lunch 80
Soup 80	Snack 80
Dinner 80	Soup 80
Day 20 80	Dinner 80
Breakfast 80	Day 24 81
Lunch 80	Breakfast 81
Snack 80	Lunch 81
Stew 80	Snack 81
Dinner 80	Stew 81
Day 21 80	Dinner 81
Breakfast 80	Day 25 81
Lunch 80	Breakfast 81
Snack 80	Lunch 81
Soup 80	Snack 81
Dinner 80	Soup 81
Week 4 80	Dinner 81
Day 22 80	Day 26 81
Breakfast 80	Breakfast 81
Lunch 80	Lunch 81
Snack 80	Snack 81
Stew 80	Stew 81
Dinner 80	Dinner 81
Day 23 80	Day 27 81

- Breakfast 81
- Lunch 81
- Snack 81
- Soup 81
- Dinner 81

Day 28 81
- Breakfast 81
- Lunch 81
- Snack 81
- Stew 81
- Dinner 82

Day 29 82
- Breakfast 82
- Lunch 82
- Snack 82
- Soup 82
- Dinner 82

Day 30 82
- Breakfast 82
- Lunch 82
- Snack 82
- Stew 82
- Dinner 82

SCIENTIFIC RECOMMENDATION: ADHD-FRIENDLY SHOPPING LIST 82
- Produce 82
- Pantry Staples 83
- Proteins 83
- Herbs and Spices 84

INTRODUCTION

Welcome to the ADHD Cookbook: Delicious Recipes for Focus and Well-being!

Living with ADHD (Attention Deficit Hyperactivity Disorder) presents unique challenges, particularly when it comes to diet and nutrition.

As someone who navigates these waters daily, I understand the importance of fueling your body with the right foods to enhance focus, maintain energy, and support overall well-being.

This cookbook is designed to be your go-to guide for creating meals that cater to the specific needs of individuals with ADHD, helping you or your loved ones thrive.

Why Diet Matters

Scientific research has shown that diet can significantly impact ADHD symptoms. Certain foods and nutrients can improve focus, mood, and energy levels, while others might exacerbate symptoms like hyperactivity and inattention.

By making mindful choices about what we eat, we can take a proactive step toward managing ADHD effectively.

What You'll Find in This Cookbook

This cookbook is more than just a collection of recipes; it's a comprehensive guide to understanding how nutrition affects ADHD. Here's what you can expect:

- Nutritional Insights: Learn about the essential nutrients that support brain health and can alleviate ADHD symptoms. Discover which foods to include and which to avoid for optimal mental clarity and focus. are designed to stabilize blood sugar levels, preventing the energy crashes and mood swings that can worsen ADHD symptoms.
- Balanced Meal Plans: To make your journey easier, I've included sample meal plans that balance protein, healthy fats, and complex carbohydrates. These meal plans
- Delicious and Easy-to-Make Recipes: Each recipe in this book is crafted to be both nutritious and delicious. From breakfast to dinner, snacks to desserts, you'll find a variety of dishes that are easy to prepare and loved by both kids and adults.
- Practical Tips for Busy Lives: Managing ADHD often means juggling many

responsibilities. I've included tips for meal prepping, shopping lists, and time-saving techniques to help you stay organized and reduce stress in the kitchen.

Empowering Your Journey

Cooking for ADHD is not just about following recipes; it's about empowering yourself with the knowledge and tools to make informed choices that benefit your health and well-being. This cookbook aims to be a resource that supports you in creating a positive and nourishing relationship with food.

Thank you for embarking on this culinary adventure with me. Let's discover together how delicious, wholesome meals can make a real difference in managing ADHD. Here's to better focus, more energy, and a healthier, happier life!

CHAPTER 1

UNDERSTANDING ADHD

Attention Deficit Hyperactivity Disorder (ADHD) is a neurodevelopmental disorder that affects millions of children and adults worldwide. Characterized by symptoms such as inattention, hyperactivity, and impulsivity, ADHD can significantly impact an individual's daily functioning, academic performance, and social relationships.

the exact cause of ADHD remains unknown, it is believed to be influenced by a combination of genetic, environmental, and neurological factors.

ADHD manifests differently in each person, with some exhibiting predominantly inattentive symptoms, others displaying hyperactive-impulsive symptoms, and many experiencing a combination of both. The diagnosis of ADHD is typically made based on a comprehensive evaluation by healthcare professionals, including behavioral assessments and clinical interviews.

History of ADHD Diet

The concept of managing ADHD symptoms through diet has a long and varied history. One of the earliest approaches was the Feingold Diet, introduced by Dr. Benjamin Feingold in the 1970s. This diet aimed to reduce hyperactivity and improve behavior by eliminating artificial food colorings, flavorings, and certain preservatives.

Although controversial and met with mixed reviews from the scientific community, the Feingold Diet sparked interest in the potential link between diet and ADHD.

Since then, numerous studies have explored the impact of various dietary components on ADHD symptoms.

Research has identified certain nutrients that may play a role in managing ADHD, such as omega-3 fatty acids, zinc, iron, magnesium, and vitamins B6 and B12.

Additionally, dietary interventions like eliminating sugar, gluten, and dairy, as well as adopting an overall balanced and nutrient-dense diet, have been investigated for their potential benefits.

In recent years, the role of gut health and the gut-brain axis in ADHD has gained attention. Emerging research suggests that the gut microbiome, the collection of microorganisms residing in the digestive tract, may influence brain function and behavior.

This has led to increased interest in dietary approaches that support gut health, such as consuming probiotics, prebiotics, and fiber-rich foods.

The Role of Nutrition in Managing ADHD Symptoms

Nutrition plays a crucial role in overall health and well-being, and it can significantly impact brain function and behavior. For individuals with ADHD, certain dietary modifications may help manage symptoms and improve quality of life. Here are several ways in which nutrition can play a role in managing ADHD:

- **Balancing Blood Sugar Levels:** Fluctuations in blood sugar levels can affect energy, concentration, and mood. Consuming balanced meals that include complex carbohydrates, protein, and healthy fats can help stabilize blood sugar levels and provide sustained energy throughout the day.
- **Supporting Neurotransmitter Production**: Neurotransmitters, such as dopamine and serotonin, are chemical messengers in the brain that regulate mood, attention, and behavior. Nutrients like omega-3 fatty acids, amino acids, and certain vitamins and minerals are essential for the production and function of neurotransmitters.
- **Reducing Inflammation**: Chronic inflammation in the body and brain has been linked to various mental health disorders, including ADHD. Anti-inflammatory foods, such as fruits, vegetables, nuts, seeds, and fatty fish, can help reduce inflammation and support brain health.
- **Improving Gut Health:** The gut-brain axis refers to the bidirectional communication between the gut and the brain. A healthy gut microbiome can positively influence brain function and behavior. Consuming probiotics, prebiotics, and fiber-rich foods can support a healthy gut microbiome.
- **Avoiding Food Triggers**: Some individuals with ADHD may be sensitive to certain foods or additives that can exacerbate symptoms. Common triggers

include artificial food colorings, preservatives, and allergens like gluten and dairy. Identifying and avoiding these triggers can help manage symptoms.

5 Benefits of an ADHD Diet

- **Enhanced Focus and Concentration**: One of the primary goals of an ADHD diet is to support brain function and improve focus and concentration. Nutrients like omega-3 fatty acids, iron, and zinc are essential for cognitive function and can help enhance attention and reduce distractibility.
- **Improved Behavior and Mood:** Diet can significantly impact mood and behavior. A balanced diet rich in whole foods, including fruits, vegetables, lean proteins, and healthy fats, can help stabilize mood and reduce irritability and impulsivity.
- **Better Sleep Quality**: Sleep disturbances are common in individuals with ADHD. Certain nutrients, such as magnesium and tryptophan, can promote relaxation and improve sleep quality. Additionally, avoiding caffeine and sugar in the evening can help prevent sleep disruptions.
- **Reduced Hyperactivity**: Some dietary components, such as artificial food colorings and sugar, can contribute to hyperactivity. By eliminating or reducing these components and focusing on nutrient-dense foods, individuals with ADHD may experience a reduction in hyperactivity.
- **Overall Health and Well-Being**: An ADHD diet emphasizes whole, nutrient-dense foods that provide essential vitamins, minerals, and antioxidants. This not only supports brain health but also promotes overall physical health and well-being, boosting energy levels and immune function.

Practical Tips for Implementing an ADHD Diet

- **Include Omega-3 Fatty Acids:** Omega-3 fatty acids, found in fatty fish (such as salmon, mackerel, and sardines), flaxseeds, chia seeds, and walnuts, are crucial for brain health. They support the production of neurotransmitters and have anti-inflammatory properties.
- **Incorporate Whole Grains:** Whole grains, such as brown rice, quinoa, and oats, provide a steady release of energy and help stabilize blood sugar levels. They are

also rich in fiber, which supports gut health.

- **Focus on Lean Proteins**: Lean proteins, such as chicken, turkey, beans, and legumes, provide essential amino acids that are building blocks for neurotransmitters. Including protein in each meal can help maintain energy levels and improve focus.

- **Add Plenty of Fruits and Vegetables:** Fruits and vegetables are rich in vitamins, minerals, and antioxidants that support overall health. They also provide fiber, which promotes gut health and helps regulate blood sugar levels.

- **Limit Processed Foods and Sugars**: Processed foods and sugars can contribute to hyperactivity and mood swings. Limiting these foods and opting for whole, unprocessed options can help manage ADHD symptoms.

- **Stay Hydrated:** Dehydration can affect concentration and energy levels. Encouraging regular water intake throughout the day can support overall cognitive function and well-being.

- **Consider Supplements:** In some cases, individuals with ADHD may benefit from supplements, such as omega-3 fatty acids, magnesium, zinc, and vitamin B6. It is important to consult with a healthcare professional before starting any supplementation.

CHAPTER 2

BREAKFAST RECIPES

Avocado and Egg Toast

Serves: 1

Cooking Time: 10 minutes

Ingredients:

- 1 slice of whole-grain bread
- 1 ripe avocado
- 1 egg
- 1 teaspoon olive oil
- Salt and pepper to taste

Instructions:

- Toast the slice of whole-grain bread until golden brown.
- While the bread is toasting, heat a small skillet over medium heat and add the olive oil.
- Crack the egg into the skillet and cook until the white is set but the yolk is still runny, about 3-4 minutes.
- While the egg is cooking, cut the avocado in half, remove the pit, and scoop out the flesh into a bowl. Mash it with a fork until smooth.
- Spread the mashed avocado on the toasted bread.
- Place the cooked egg on top of the avocado toast.
- Season with salt and pepper to taste.
- Serve immediately.

Scientific Note:

- **Whole-grain bread**: Provides a steady release of glucose, which helps maintain concentration and energy levels without causing spikes and crashes in blood sugar.
- **Avocado:** Rich in healthy fats and folate, avocados support brain function and can help stabilize mood and behavior.
- **Eggs**: High in protein and essential fatty acids, eggs contribute to sustained energy and cognitive function, which can help manage ADHD symptoms.

- **Olive oil:** Contains monounsaturated fats and antioxidants that support brain health and reduce inflammation.

Nutritional Information (Approximate):

- Calories: 320
- Protein: 10g
- Carbohydrates: 26g
- Fiber: 8g
- Sugars: 2g
- Fat: 22g (Healthy fats)

Banana and Almond Butter Smoothie

Serves: 1

Cooking Time: 5 minutes

Ingredients:

- 1 banana
- 1 tablespoon almond butter
- 1 cup unsweetened almond milk
- 1 tablespoon chia seeds
- 1/2 teaspoon cinnamon

Instructions:

- Peel the banana and cut it into chunks.
- Place the banana, almond butter, almond milk, chia seds, and cinnamon in a blender.
- Blend until smooth and creamy.
- Pour the smoothie into a glass and serve immediately.

Scientific Note:

- **Banana:** Provides natural sugars and fiber for sustained energy release, along with potassium, which supports brain function.
- **Almond butter:** Rich in protein, healthy fats, and magnesium, which can help with neurotransmitter function and reduce hyperactivity.
- **Almond milk:** A good source of vitamin E and healthy fats, almond milk supports brain health and reduces inflammation.
- **Chia seeds:** High in omega-3 fatty acids, which are essential for brain health and can help manage ADHD symptoms.

- **Cinnamon**: Contains antioxidants that help stabilize blood sugar levels, which can prevent mood swings and hyperactivity.

Nutritional Information (Approximate):

- Calories: 300
- Protein: 8g
- Carbohydrates: 38g
- Fiber: 10g
- Sugars: 15g (Natural sugars from banana)
- Fat: 14g (Healthy fats)

Greek Yogurt Parfait

Serves: 1

Cooking Time: 5 minutes

Ingredients:

- 1 cup plain Greek yogurt
- 1/2 cup mixed berries (blueberries, raspberries, strawberries)
- 2 tablespoons pumpkin seeds
- 1 tablespoon honey
- 1/2 teaspoon vanilla extract
- Instructions:
- In a bowl, mix the plain Greek yogurt with honey and vanilla extract.
- Layer the yogurt mixture in a glass or bowl.
- Add a layer of mixed berries on top of the yogurt.
- Sprinkle pumpkin seeds over the berries.
- Serve immediately.

Scientific Note:

- **Greek yogurt:** High in protein and probiotics, which can improve gut health and have a positive impact on brain function.
- **Berries:** Rich in antioxidants and vitamins, which support cognitive function and reduce inflammation.
- **Pumpkin seeds:** A good source of magnesium and omega-3 fatty acids, which are essential for brain health and can help reduce hyperactivity.
- **Honey:** Provides natural sweetness without causing blood sugar spikes.

Nutritional Information (Approximate):

- Calories: 250
- Protein: 20g
- Carbohydrates: 30g
- Fiber: 5g
- Sugars: 18g (Natural sugars from honey and berries)
- Fat: 8g (Healthy fats)

Sweet Potato and Spinach Hash

Serves: 1

Cooking Time: 20 minutes

Ingredients:

- 1 medium sweet potato, peeled and diced
- 1 cup fresh spinach
- 1/2 small red onion, finely chopped
- 1 tablespoon olive oil
- 1 clove garlic, minced
- Salt and pepper to taste

Instructions:

- Heat the olive oil in a skillet over medium heat.
- Add the diced sweet potato and cook for about 10 minutes, stirring occasionally, until the sweet potato is tender.
- Add the chopped red onion and minced garlic to the skillet and cook for another 5 minutes, until the onion is translucent.
- Add the fresh spinach to the skillet and cook until wilted, about 2 minutes.
- Season with salt and pepper to taste.
- Serve immediately.

Scientific Note:

- **Sweet potato:** High in fiber and complex carbohydrates, providing a steady release of energy and helping to maintain concentration.
- **Spinach:** Rich in iron, magnesium, and folate, which are essential for brain health and cognitive function.
- **Red onion:** Contains antioxidants and vitamins that support brain health.
- **Garlic:** Known for its anti-inflammatory properties, which can help reduce inflammation in the brain.

Nutritional Information (Approximate):

- Calories: 180
- Protein: 3g
- Carbohydrates: 30g
- Fiber: 5g
- Sugars: 7g (Natural sugars from sweet potato)
- Fat: 7g (Healthy fats)

Quinoa Breakfast Bowl

Serves: 1

Cooking Time: 20 minutes

Ingredients:

- 1/2 cup cooked quinoa
- 1/4 cup diced mango
- 1/4 cup diced kiwi
- 2 tablespoons unsweetened shredded coconut
- 1 tablespoon chia seeds
- 1/2 cup unsweetened coconut milk
- 1 teaspoon honey

Instructions:

- Cook quinoa according to package instructions and let it cool.
- In a bowl, combine cooked quinoa, diced mango, diced kiwi, and unsweetened shredded coconut.
- Sprinkle chia seeds on top.
- Pour unsweetened coconut milk over the mixture.
- Drizzle with honey.
- Serve immediately.

Scientific Note:

- **Quinoa**: High in protein and essential amino acids, quinoa supports cognitive function and provides a steady source of energy.
- **Mango and kiwi:** Rich in vitamins, antioxidants, and fiber, these fruits help improve brain function and reduce inflammation.
- **Shredded coconut**: Provides healthy fats that support brain health.
- **Chia seeds**: High in omega-3 fatty acids, which are essential for brain health and can help manage ADHD symptoms.

- **Coconut milk**: Contains healthy fats that support brain function and reduce inflammation.

Nutritional Information (Approximate):

- Calories: 320
- Protein: 8g
- Carbohydrates: 45g
- Fiber: 8g
- Sugars: 15g (Natural sugars from fruits)
- Fat: 14g (Healthy fats)

Veggie Omelette with Goat Cheese

Serves: 1

Cooking Time: 15 minutes

Ingredients:

- 2 large eggs
- 1/4 cup diced bell peppers (red, green, or yellow)
- 1/4 cup diced zucchini
- 1/4 cup baby spinach
- 2 tablespoons crumbled goat cheese
- 1 tablespoon olive oil
- Salt and pepper to taste

Instructions:

- Heat olive oil in a skillet over medium heat.
- Add diced bell peppers and zucchini to the skillet, cooking for about 5 minutes until they soften.
- Add baby spinach to the skillet and cook until wilted, about 2 minutes.
- In a bowl, whisk the eggs with a pinch of salt and pepper.
- Pour the eggs over the vegetables in the skillet.
- Cook until the eggs are set, about 5 minutes.
- Sprinkle crumbled goat cheese over the omelette.
- Fold the omelette in half and serve immediately.

Scientific Note:

- **Eggs**: High in protein and essential fatty acids, eggs contribute to sustained energy and cognitive function.
- **Bell peppers and zucchini**: Rich in vitamins and antioxidants, these vegetables support brain health and reduce inflammation.
- **Baby spinach:** High in iron, magnesium, and folate, which are essential for brain health and cognitive function.
- **Goat cheese:** Provides protein and healthy fats that support brain function.
- **Olive oil**: Contains monounsaturated fats and antioxidants that support brain health and reduce inflammation.

Nutritional Information (Approximate):

- Calories: 300
- Protein: 16g
- Carbohydrates: 10g
- Fiber: 3g
- Sugars: 4g (Natural sugars from vegetables)
- Fat: 23g (Healthy fats)

Chickpea Pancakes with Spinach and Tomato

Serves: 1

Cooking Time: 15 minutes

Ingredients:

- 1/2 cup chickpea flour
- 1/4 cup water
- 1/4 cup chopped spinach
- 1 small tomato, diced
- 1/2 teaspoon turmeric
- 1/4 teaspoon cumin
- Salt and pepper to taste
- 1 tablespoon olive oil

Instructions:

- In a bowl, mix chickpea flour, water, turmeric, cumin, salt, and pepper until smooth.

- Fold in chopped spinach and diced tomato.
- Heat olive oil in a non-stick skillet over medium heat.
- Pour the batter into the skillet, spreading it evenly to form a pancake.
- Cook for about 3-4 minutes on each side, until golden brown and cooked through.
- Serve immediately.

Scientific Note:

- **Chickpea flour:** High in protein and fiber, chickpea flour provides steady energy release and supports cognitive function.
- **Spinach**: Rich in iron, magnesium, and folate, spinach aids in brain health and reduces inflammation.
- **Tomato**: Contains antioxidants such as lycopene, which support brain health.
- **Turmeric:** Contains curcumin, which has anti-inflammatory properties and can enhance brain function.
- **Cumin**: Contains antioxidants that support overall health.

Nutritional Information (Approximate):

- Calories: 250
- Protein: 10g
- Carbohydrates: 35g
- Fiber: 7g
- Sugars: 4g (Natural sugars from vegetables)
- Fat: 10g (Healthy fats)

Baked Sweet Potato and Black Bean Hash

Serves: 1

Cooking Time: 30 minutes

Ingredients:

- 1 small sweet potato, peeled and diced
- 1/2 cup black beans, rinsed and drained
- 1/4 red onion, finely chopped
- 1/4 red bell pepper, diced
- 1 tablespoon olive oil
- 1/2 teaspoon paprika
- 1/2 teaspoon cumin
- Salt and pepper to taste
- Fresh cilantro for garnish (optional)

Instructions:

- Preheat oven to 400°F (200°C).
- In a bowl, toss diced sweet potato with olive oil, paprika, cumin, salt, and pepper.
- Spread the sweet potato on a baking sheet and bake for 20 minutes, or until tender.
- In a skillet, sauté red onion and red bell pepper over medium heat until softened, about 5 minutes.
- Add black beans to the skillet and cook for another 3-4 minutes.
- Combine the roasted sweet potato with the black bean mixture.
- Serve warm, garnished with fresh cilantro if desired.

Scientific Note:

- **Sweet potato**: Provides complex carbohydrates and fiber, which support steady energy levels and cognitive function.
- **Black beans:** High in protein and fiber, black beans help maintain steady blood sugar levels and support brain health.
- **Red bell pepper**: Rich in vitamin C and antioxidants, red bell peppers support overall health and cognitive function.
- **Red onion:** Contains antioxidants and vitamins that support brain health.
- **Paprika and cumin**: Contain antioxidants that help reduce inflammation and support overall health.

Nutritional Information (Approximate):

- Calories: 300
- Protein: 8g
- Carbohydrates: 50g
- Fiber: 12g
- Sugars: 8g (Natural sugars from vegetables)
- Fat: 8g (Healthy fats)

Smoked Salmon and Avocado Wrap

Serves: 1

Cooking Time: 10 minutes

Ingredients:

- 1 whole-grain tortilla

- 2 oz smoked salmon
- 1/2 avocado, sliced
- 1/4 cucumber, thinly sliced
- 1 tablespoon hummus
- A handful of arugula
- Fresh dill for garnish (optional)

Instructions:

- Lay the whole-grain tortilla flat on a plate.
- Spread the hummus evenly over the tortilla.
- Layer the smoked salmon, avocado slices, cucumber slices, and arugula on top.
- Roll up the tortilla tightly to form a wrap.
- Slice the wrap in half and garnish with fresh dill if desired.
- Serve immediately.

Scientific Note:

- **Smoked salmon:** Rich in omega-3 fatty acids, which are essential for brain health and can help manage ADHD symptoms.
- **Avocado:** Contains healthy fats and folate, supporting brain function and mood stabilization.
- **Cucumber:** Provides hydration and antioxidants that support overall health.
- **Hummus:** Made from chickpeas, it provides protein and fiber for steady energy release.
- **Arugula:** Contains vitamins and minerals that support cognitive function.

Nutritional Information (Approximate):

- Calories: 350
- Protein: 16g
- Carbohydrates: 28g
- Fiber: 10g
- Sugars: 2g (Natural sugars from vegetables)
- Fat: 20g (Healthy fats)

Apple Cinnamon Quinoa Porridge

Serves: 1

Cooking Time: 20 minutes

Ingredients:

- 1/4 cup quinoa, rinsed
- 1/2 cup unsweetened almond milk
- 1/2 apple, diced

- 1 tablespoon raisins
- 1/2 teaspoon cinnamon
- 1/4 teaspoon nutmeg
- 1 teaspoon maple syrup
- 1 tablespoon chopped walnuts

Instructions:

- In a small saucepan, combine quinoa and almond milk. Bring to a boil.
- Reduce heat to low, cover, and simmer for about 15 minutes, or until the quinoa is tender and the liquid is absorbed.
- Stir in the diced apple, raisins, cinnamon, and nutmeg. Cook for another 3-5 minutes, until the apple is tender.
- Remove from heat and stir in the maple syrup.
- Transfer to a bowl and top with chopped walnuts.
- Serve warm.

Scientific Note:

- **Quinoa**: High in protein and fiber, quinoa provides steady energy and supports cognitive function.
- **Apple**: Contains fiber and natural sugars for a slow release of energy.
- **Raisins**: Provide natural sweetness and are rich in antioxidants.
- **Cinnamon**: Helps stabilize blood sugar levels, which can prevent mood swings and hyperactivity.
- **Walnuts**: Rich in omega-3 fatty acids, which support brain health and reduce inflammation.

Nutritional Information (Approximate):

- Calories: 320
- Protein: 8g
- Carbohydrates: 50g
- Fiber: 7g
- Sugars: 15g (Natural sugars from fruit)
- Fat: 10g (Healthy fats)

CHAPTER 3

LUNCH RECIPES

Grilled Chicken and Quinoa Salad

Serves: 1

Cooking Time: 25 minutes

Ingredients:

- 1/2 cup cooked quinoa
- 1 grilled chicken breast, sliced
- 1/2 cup cherry tomatoes, halved
- 1/4 cup diced cucumber
- 1/4 cup shredded carrots
- 1 tablespoon pumpkin seeds
- 2 tablespoons extra virgin olive oil
- 1 tablespoon lemon juice
- Salt and pepper to taste

Instructions:

- Cook quinoa according to package instructions and let it cool.
- Season the chicken breast with salt and pepper, then grill until fully cooked and slice it.
- In a large bowl, combine cooked quinoa, cherry tomatoes, cucumber, shredded carrots, and pumpkin seeds.
- Add the grilled chicken slices to the salad.
- In a small bowl, whisk together the olive oil and lemon juice, then pour over the salad.
- Toss the salad to combine all ingredients evenly.
- Serve immediately.

Scientific Note:

- **Quinoa**: High in protein and fiber, quinoa provides steady energy release and supports cognitive function.
- **Grilled chicken**: Provides lean protein essential for maintaining muscle mass and energy levels, contributing to better focus.
- **Cherry tomatoes**: Rich in antioxidants, including lycopene, which supports brain health.
- **Cucumber**: Hydrating and contains antioxidants that support overall health.

- **Carrots**: High in beta-carotene, which supports brain health and reduces inflammation.
- **Pumpkin seeds**: Rich in magnesium and omega-3 fatty acids, which are essential for brain health and reducing hyperactivity.
- **Olive oil:** Contains monounsaturated fats and antioxidants that support brain health and reduce inflammation.

Nutritional Information (Approximate):

- Calories: 400
- Protein: 30g
- Carbohydrates: 35g
- Fiber: 8g
- Sugars: 6g (Natural sugars from vegetables)
- Fat: 18g (Healthy fats)

Lentil and Vegetable Stir-Fry

Serves: 1

Cooking Time: 20 minutes

Ingredients:

- 1/2 cup cooked lentils
- 1/4 cup diced bell peppers (red, yellow, green)
- 1/4 cup broccoli florets
- 1/4 cup snap peas
- 1 small carrot, thinly sliced
- 1 clove garlic, minced
- 1 tablespoon olive oil
- 2 tablespoons tahini
- 1 tablespoon lemon juice
- 1 tablespoon water
- Salt and pepper to taste

Instructions:

- Cook lentils according to package instructions and set aside.
- In a large skillet, heat olive oil over medium heat.
- Add minced garlic and sauté for about 1 minute until fragrant.
- Add bell peppers, broccoli, snap peas, and carrot to the skillet. Cook for about 5-7 minutes until vegetables are tender.
- Add the cooked lentils to the skillet and stir to combine.

- In a small bowl, whisk together tahini, lemon juice, and water until smooth.
- Pour the tahini dressing over the stir-fry and mix well.
- Season with salt and pepper to taste.
- Serve immediately.

Scientific Note:

- **Lentils**: High in protein and fiber, lentils provide sustained energy and help maintain stable blood sugar levels.
- **Bell peppers:** Rich in vitamin C and antioxidants, supporting overall health and cognitive function.
- **Broccoli**: Contains antioxidants and nutrients that support brain health and reduce inflammation.
- **Snap peas:** Provide fiber and vitamins that support overall health.
- **Carrots**: High in beta-carotene, which supports brain health and reduces inflammation.
- **Garlic:** Known for its anti-inflammatory properties, which can help reduce inflammation in the brain.
- **Tahini**: Made from sesame seeds, tahini is rich in healthy fats and magnesium, which support brain health.
- **Olive oil:** Contains monounsaturated fats and antioxidants that support brain health and reduce inflammation.

Nutritional Information (Approximate):

- Calories: 350
- Protein: 18g
- Carbohydrates: 40g
- Fiber: 12g
- Sugars: 10g (Natural sugars from vegetables)
- Fat: 14g (Healthy fats)

Turkey and Avocado Lettuce Wraps

Serves: 1

Cooking Time: 10 minutes

Ingredients:

- 4 large romaine lettuce leaves
- 4 slices of roasted turkey breast
- 1/2 avocado, sliced
- 1/4 red bell pepper, sliced
- 1/4 cucumber, julienned
- 1 tablespoon hummus
- 1 teaspoon lemon juice
- Salt and pepper to taste

Instructions:

- Lay out the romaine lettuce leaves on a plate.
- Spread a thin layer of hummus on each leaf.
- Place a slice of roasted turkey breast on each lettuce leaf.
- Top with avocado slices, red bell pepper slices, and julienned cucumber.
- Drizzle with lemon juice and season with salt and pepper.
- Roll up the lettuce leaves to form wraps.
- Serve immediately.

Scientific Note:

- **Turkey**: A good source of lean protein and tryptophan, which can help with serotonin production and improve mood.
- **Avocado**: Contains healthy fats and folate, supporting brain function and mood stabilization.
- **Red bell pepper**: Rich in vitamin C and antioxidants, supporting cognitive function.
- **Cucumber**: Provides hydration and antioxidants that support overall health.
- **Hummus:** Made from chickpeas, it provides protein and fiber for steady energy release.
- **Romaine lettuce**: Low in calories and high in vitamins, supporting overall health.

Nutritional Information (Approximate):

- Calories: 250
- Protein: 20g
- Carbohydrates: 15g
- Fiber: 7g
- Sugars: 4g (Natural sugars from vegetables)
- Fat: 14g (Healthy fats)

Salmon and Quinoa Stuffed Peppers

Serves: 1

Cooking Time: 30 minutes

Ingredients:

- 1 large bell pepper (any color)
- 1/2 cup cooked quinoa
- 1/4 cup cooked salmon, flaked
- 1/4 cup diced zucchini
- 1/4 cup diced tomatoes
- 1 tablespoon chopped parsley
- 1 tablespoon olive oil
- 1/2 teaspoon garlic powder
- Salt and pepper to taste

Instructions:

- Preheat the oven to 375°F (190°C).
- Cut the top off the bell pepper and remove the seeds and membranes.
- In a bowl, combine cooked quinoa, flaked salmon, diced zucchini, diced tomatoes, parsley, olive oil, garlic powder, salt, and pepper.
- Stuff the bell pepper with the quinoa and salmon mixture.
- Place the stuffed pepper in a baking dish and bake for 20-25 minutes, until the pepper is tender.
- Serve immediately.

Scientific Note:

- **Salmon:** Rich in omega-3 fatty acids, which are essential for brain health and can help manage ADHD symptoms.
- **Quinoa**: High in protein and fiber, providing steady energy and supporting cognitive function.
- **Bell pepper:** Contains antioxidants and vitamins that support overall health and cognitive function.
- **Zucchini:** Provides vitamins and minerals that support brain health and reduce inflammation.
- **Tomatoes:** Rich in lycopene and other antioxidants that support brain health.

- **Olive oil:** Contains monounsaturated fats and antioxidants that support brain health and reduce inflammation.

Nutritional Information (Approximate):

- Calories: 300
- Protein: 20g
- Carbohydrates: 35g
- Fiber: 8g
- Sugars: 7g (Natural sugars from vegetables)
- Fat: 10g (Healthy fats)

Chickpea and Spinach Salad

Serves: 1

Cooking Time: 10 minutes

Ingredients:

- 1 cup cooked chickpeas
- 2 cups fresh spinach leaves
- 1/4 cup shredded carrots
- 1/4 cup cherry tomatoes, halved
- 2 tablespoons sunflower seeds
- 1 tablespoon apple cider vinegar
- 2 tablespoons extra virgin olive oil
- 1 teaspoon Dijon mustard
- Salt and pepper to taste

Instructions:

- In a large bowl, combine chickpeas, spinach leaves, shredded carrots, cherry tomatoes, and sunflower seeds.
- In a small bowl, whisk together apple cider vinegar, olive oil, Dijon mustard, salt, and pepper.
- Pour the dressing over the salad and toss to combine.
- Serve immediately.

Scientific Note:

- **Chickpeas**: High in protein and fiber, chickpeas provide steady energy and support cognitive function.
- **Spinach**: Rich in iron, magnesium, and folate, spinach aids in brain health and reduces inflammation.
- **Carrots**: High in beta-carotene, which supports brain health and reduces inflammation.

- **Cherry tomatoes:** Rich in antioxidants, including lycopene, which supports brain health.
- **Sunflower seeds:** A good source of vitamin E and healthy fats that support brain function.
- **Olive oil:** Contains monounsaturated fats and antioxidants that support brain health and reduce inflammation.

Nutritional Information (Approximate):

- Calories: 350
- Protein: 14g
- Carbohydrates: 30g
- Fiber: 10g
- Sugars: 6g (Natural sugars from vegetables)
- Fat: 18g (Healthy fats)

Lentil and Vegetable Soup

Serves: 1

Cooking Time: 30 minutes

Ingredients:

- 1/2 cup dried lentils, rinsed
- 1 small carrot, diced
- 1/2 celery stalk, diced
- 1/2 onion, diced
- 1 garlic clove, minced
- 1 small zucchini, diced
- 2 cups low-sodium vegetable broth
- 1 tablespoon olive oil
- 1/2 teaspoon cumin
- 1/2 teaspoon turmeric
- Salt and pepper to taste
- Fresh parsley for garnish (optional)

Instructions:

- In a large pot, heat olive oil over medium heat.
- Add diced carrot, celery, and onion. Sauté for about 5 minutes until vegetables are softened.
- Add minced garlic and cook for another minute.
- Add rinsed lentils, diced zucchini, and vegetable broth to the pot.
- Stir in cumin, turmeric, salt, and pepper.
- Bring to a boil, then reduce heat and simmer for 20-25 minutes until lentils and vegetables are tender.
- Adjust seasoning if needed.

- Garnish with fresh parsley if desired and serve hot.

Scientific Note:

- **Lentils**: High in protein and fiber, lentils provide sustained energy and help maintain stable blood sugar levels.
- **Carrots**: Rich in beta-carotene, supporting brain health and reducing inflammation.
- **Celery**: Contains antioxidants and vitamins that support overall health.
- **Onion**: Contains antioxidants and vitamins that support brain health.
- **Garlic**: Known for its anti-inflammatory properties, which can help reduce inflammation in the brain.
- **Zucchini**: Provides vitamins and minerals that support brain health and reduce inflammation.
- **Olive oil:** Contains monounsaturated fats and antioxidants that support brain health and reduce inflammation.

Nutritional Information (Approximate):

- Calories: 300
- Protein: 16g
- Carbohydrates: 40g
- Fiber: 12g
- Sugars: 7g (Natural sugars from vegetables)
- Fat: 10g (Healthy fats)

Butternut Squash and Black Bean Tacos

Serves: 1

Cooking Time: 25 minutes

Ingredients:

- 1/2 small butternut squash, peeled and diced
- 1/2 cup cooked black beans
- 1/4 red onion, thinly sliced
- 1/2 avocado, diced
- 1/4 cup fresh cilantro, chopped
- 1 teaspoon cumin
- 1/2 teaspoon smoked paprika
- 1 tablespoon olive oil
- 2 small corn tortillas
- Salt and pepper to taste
- Lime wedges for serving

Instructions:

- Preheat the oven to 400°F (200°C).
- Toss the diced butternut squash with olive oil, cumin, smoked paprika, salt, and pepper. Spread on a baking sheet and roast for 20 minutes, or until tender.
- In a small pan, warm the corn tortillas over medium heat until they are pliable.
- In a bowl, combine the roasted butternut squash, cooked black beans, and red onion.
- Divide the mixture between the two tortillas.
- Top with diced avocado and fresh cilantro.
- Serve with lime wedges.

Scientific Note:

- **Butternut squash:** Rich in vitamins A and C, which support brain health and reduce inflammation.
- **Black beans:** High in protein and fiber, providing sustained energy and supporting cognitive function.
- **Avocado:** Contains healthy fats and folate, supporting brain function and mood stabilization.
- **Red onion:** Provides antioxidants and vitamins that support brain health.
- **Cilantro:** Contains antioxidants and can help detoxify the body.

Nutritional Information (Approximate):

- Calories: 350
- Protein: 12g
- Carbohydrates: 50g
- Fiber: 14g
- Sugars: 8g (Natural sugars from vegetables)
- Fat: 15g (Healthy fats)

Quinoa and Edamame Salad

Serves: 1

Cooking Time: 20 minutes

Ingredients:

- 1/2 cup cooked quinoa
- 1/2 cup shelled edamame (cooked)
- 1/4 cup shredded red cabbage
- 1/4 cup shredded carrot

- 1/4 cup diced cucumber
- 2 tablespoons chopped green onions
- 1 tablespoon sesame seeds
- 1 tablespoon rice vinegar
- 1 tablespoon sesame oil
- 1 teaspoon soy sauce (gluten-free if needed)
- Salt and pepper to taste

Instructions:

- Cook quinoa according to package instructions and let it cool.
- In a large bowl, combine cooked quinoa, edamame, shredded red cabbage, shredded carrot, diced cucumber, and green onions.
- In a small bowl, whisk together rice vinegar, sesame oil, soy sauce, salt, and pepper.
- Pour the dressing over the quinoa mixture and toss to combine.
- Sprinkle with sesame seeds.
- Serve immediately.

Scientific Note:

- Quinoa: High in protein and fiber, providing steady energy and supporting cognitive function.
- Edamame: Rich in protein, fiber, and omega-3 fatty acids, supporting brain health and reducing inflammation.
- Red cabbage: Contains antioxidants and vitamins that support brain health and reduce inflammation.
- Carrot: High in beta-carotene, which supports brain health and reduces inflammation.
- Cucumber: Provides hydration and antioxidants that support overall health.
- Sesame oil: Contains healthy fats that support brain function.

Nutritional Information (Approximate):

- Calories: 300
- Protein: 15g
- Carbohydrates: 35g
- Fiber: 10g
- Sugars: 5g (Natural sugars from vegetables)
- Fat: 12g (Healthy fats)

Grilled Portobello Mushroom and Quinoa Bowl

Serves: 1

Cooking Time: 25 minutes

Ingredients:

- 1 large Portobello mushroom cap
- 1/2 cup cooked quinoa
- 1/4 cup chickpeas, rinsed and drained
- 1/4 cup diced bell pepper (any color)
- 1/4 cup diced cucumber
- 2 tablespoons chopped fresh parsley
- 1 tablespoon balsamic vinegar
- 1 tablespoon olive oil
- 1 clove garlic, minced
- Salt and pepper to taste

Instructions:

- Preheat the grill to medium-high heat.
- In a small bowl, mix balsamic vinegar, olive oil, minced garlic, salt, and pepper. Brush the mixture on the Portobello mushroom cap.
- Grill the mushroom for about 5-7 minutes on each side, until tender.
- While the mushroom is grilling, combine cooked quinoa, chickpeas, bell pepper, cucumber, and parsley in a bowl.
- Slice the grilled Portobello mushroom and place it on top of the quinoa mixture.
- Serve immediately.

Scientific Note:

- Portobello mushroom: Rich in B vitamins and antioxidants, supporting brain health and reducing inflammation.
- Quinoa: High in protein and fiber, providing steady energy and supporting cognitive function.
- Chickpeas: Provide protein and fiber, which help maintain stable blood sugar levels and support cognitive function.
- Bell pepper: Contains vitamins and antioxidants that support brain health and reduce inflammation.
- Cucumber: Provides hydration and antioxidants that support overall health.
- Parsley: Contains antioxidants and vitamins that support overall health.

Nutritional Information (Approximate):

- Calories: 350
- Protein: 12g
- Carbohydrates: 45g
- Fiber: 10g
- Sugars: 6g (Natural sugars from vegetables)
- Fat: 15g (Healthy fats)

Zucchini Noodles with Pesto and Grilled Shrimp

Serves: 1

Cooking Time: 20 minutes

Ingredients:

- 1 medium zucchini, spiralized into noodles
- 6 large shrimp, peeled and deveined
- 2 tablespoons homemade pesto (see below)
- 1 tablespoon olive oil
- 1/4 cup cherry tomatoes, halved
- 1 tablespoon pine nuts
- Salt and pepper to taste
- For the Pesto:
- 1 cup fresh basil leaves
- 1/4 cup pine nuts
- 1 clove garlic
- 1/4 cup olive oil
- Salt and pepper to taste

Instructions:

- To make the pesto, blend basil leaves, pine nuts, garlic, olive oil, salt, and pepper in a food processor until smooth.
- In a skillet, heat olive oil over medium heat. Add the shrimp, season with salt and pepper, and cook for 2-3 minutes on each side until they are pink and opaque. Remove from the skillet and set aside.
- In the same skillet, add the spiralized zucchini noodles and cook for 2-3 minutes until tender.
- Toss the zucchini noodles with 2 tablespoons of pesto.
- Add cherry tomatoes and grilled shrimp to the skillet and toss to combine.

- Serve the zucchini noodles topped with pine nuts.

Scientific Note:

- Zucchini: Low in calories and high in vitamins and minerals, supporting overall health and hydration.
- Shrimp: High in protein and omega-3 fatty acids, supporting brain health and cognitive function.
- Basil: Contains antioxidants and essential oils that support overall health.
- Pine nuts: Provide healthy fats and magnesium, which support brain health.
- Cherry tomatoes: Rich in vitamins and antioxidants that support brain health.

Nutritional Information (Approximate):

- Calories: 300
- Protein: 20g
- Carbohydrates: 12g
- Fiber: 4g
- Sugars: 6g (Natural sugars from vegetables)
- Fat: 20g (Healthy fats)

CHAPTER 4

SNACKS AND DIPS

Carrot Sticks with Tahini Dip

Serves: 1

Cooking Time: 10 minutes

Ingredients:

- 2 large carrots, peeled and cut into sticks
- 2 tablespoons tahini
- 1 tablespoon lemon juice
- 1 clove garlic, minced
- 1 tablespoon water
- Salt and pepper to taste
- 1 teaspoon olive oil
- 1/4 teaspoon ground cumin

Instructions:

- In a small bowl, combine tahini, lemon juice, minced garlic, water, olive oil, ground cumin, salt, and pepper.
- Mix well until smooth. Add more water if needed to achieve desired consistency.
- Arrange the carrot sticks on a plate.
- Serve the tahini dip alongside the carrot sticks.

Scientific Note:

- **Carrots**: High in beta-carotene, which supports brain health and reduces inflammation.
- **Tahini**: Made from sesame seeds, it is rich in healthy fats and magnesium, which support brain health and cognitive function.
- **Garlic**: Known for its anti-inflammatory properties, which can help reduce inflammation in the brain.
- **Olive oil:** Contains monounsaturated fats and antioxidants that support brain health and reduce inflammation.

Nutritional Information (Approximate):

- Calories: 200
- Protein: 4g
- Carbohydrates: 18g
- Fiber: 6g
- Sugars: 9g (Natural sugars from carrots)
- Fat: 14g (Healthy fats)

Cucumber Slices with Avocado Dip

Serves: 1

Cooking Time: 10 minutes

Ingredients:

- 1 cucumber, sliced
- 1/2 avocado
- 1 tablespoon lime juice
- 1 clove garlic, minced
- 1 tablespoon chopped fresh cilantro
- Salt and pepper to taste

Instructions:

- In a small bowl, mash the avocado until smooth.

- Add lime juice, minced garlic, chopped cilantro, salt, and pepper to the mashed avocado. Mix well.
- Arrange the cucumber slices on a plate.
- Serve the avocado dip alongside the cucumber slices.

Scientific Note:

- **Cucumber**: Provides hydration and antioxidants that support overall health and brain function.
- **Avocado**: Contains healthy fats and folate, which support brain function and mood stabilization.
- **Lime juice**: High in vitamin C and antioxidants, supporting overall health.
- **Cilantro**: Contains antioxidants and vitamins that support overall health.
- **Garlic**: Known for its anti-inflammatory properties, which can help reduce inflammation in the brain.

Nutritional Information (Approximate):

- Calories: 180
- Protein: 2g
- Carbohydrates: 16g
- Fiber: 8g
- Sugars: 5g (Natural sugars from cucumber)
- Fat: 14g (Healthy fats)

Celery Sticks with Almond Butter Dip

Serves: 1

Cooking Time: 5 minutes

Ingredients:

- 2 celery stalks, cut into sticks
- 2 tablespoons almond butter
- 1 teaspoon honey
- 1/4 teaspoon cinnamon

Instructions:

- In a small bowl, mix almond butter, honey, and cinnamon until well combined.
- Arrange the celery sticks on a plate.
- Serve the almond butter dip alongside the celery sticks.

Scientific Note:

- **Celery**: Low in calories and high in water content, providing hydration and essential vitamins.
- **Almond butter:** Rich in healthy fats, protein, and magnesium, supporting brain health and reducing inflammation.
- **Honey**: Natural sweetener that provides antioxidants and helps maintain steady blood sugar levels.
- **Cinnamon**: Contains antioxidants and helps stabilize blood sugar levels, which can prevent mood swings and hyperactivity.

Nutritional Information (Approximate):

- Calories: 210
- Protein: 6g
- Carbohydrates: 15g
- Fiber: 4g
- Sugars: 10g (Natural sugars from honey)
- Fat: 16g (Healthy fats)

Bell Pepper Strips with Hummus

Serves: 1

Cooking Time: 5 minutes

Ingredients:

- 1 bell pepper (any color), cut into strips
- 1/4 cup hummus
- 1 teaspoon lemon juice
- 1/4 teaspoon smoked paprika
- Salt and pepper to taste

Instructions:

- In a small bowl, mix hummus, lemon juice, smoked paprika, salt, and pepper until well combined.
- Arrange the bell pepper strips on a plate.
- Serve the hummus dip alongside the bell pepper strips.

Scientific Note:

- **Bell peppers**: High in vitamin C and antioxidants, supporting cognitive function and reducing inflammation.
- **Hummus**: Made from chickpeas, it provides protein and fiber for steady energy release.
- **Lemon juice**: High in vitamin C and antioxidants, supporting overall health.
- **Smoked paprika**: Adds flavor and contains antioxidants that support overall health.

Nutritional Information (Approximate):

- Calories: 150
- Protein: 5g
- Carbohydrates: 18g
- Fiber: 6g
- Sugars: 6g (Natural sugars from bell pepper)
- Fat: 8g (Healthy fats)

Apple Slices with Sunflower Seed Butter Dip

Serves: 1

Cooking Time: 5 minutes

Ingredients:

- 1 apple, sliced
- 2 tablespoons sunflower seed butter
- 1/2 teaspoon ground flaxseed
- 1/4 teaspoon ground cinnamon

Instructions:

- Slice the apple and arrange the slices on a plate.
- In a small bowl, mix sunflower seed butter, ground flaxseed, and ground cinnamon until well combined.
- Serve the sunflower seed butter dip alongside the apple slices.

Scientific Note:

- **Apple**: Provides fiber and natural sugars for a steady energy release and supports cognitive function.
- **Sunflower seed butter:** Rich in healthy fats, protein, and vitamin E, which supports brain health and reduces inflammation.
- **Flaxseed:** High in omega-3 fatty acids and fiber, which support brain health and cognitive function.
- **Cinnamon**: Contains antioxidants and helps stabilize blood sugar levels, which can prevent mood swings and hyperactivity.

Nutritional Information (Approximate):

- Calories: 250
- Protein: 5g
- Carbohydrates: 30g
- Fiber: 6g
- Sugars: 20g (Natural sugars from apple)
- Fat: 14g (Healthy fats)

Jicama Sticks with Guacamole

Serves: 1

Cooking Time: 10 minutes

Ingredients:

- 1 small jicama, peeled and cut into sticks
- 1/2 avocado
- 1 tablespoon lime juice
- 1 small garlic clove, minced
- 1 tablespoon chopped fresh cilantro
- Salt and pepper to taste

Instructions:

- Peel and cut the jicama into sticks and arrange them on a plate.
- In a small bowl, mash the avocado until smooth.

- Add lime juice, minced garlic, chopped cilantro, salt, and pepper to the mashed avocado. Mix well.
- Serve the guacamole dip alongside the jicama sticks.

Scientific Note:

- **Jicama**: Low in calories and high in fiber, providing hydration and essential vitamins.
- **Avocado**: Contains healthy fats and folate, which support brain function and mood stabilization.
- **Lime juice**: High in vitamin C and antioxidants, supporting overall health.
- **Garlic**: Known for its anti-inflammatory properties, which can help reduce inflammation in the brain.
- **Cilantro**: Contains antioxidants and vitamins that support overall health.

Nutritional Information (Approximate):

- Calories: 200
- Protein: 2g
- Carbohydrates: 28g
- Fiber: 12g
- Sugars: 6g (Natural sugars from jicama)
- Fat: 14g (Healthy fats)

Radish Slices with Beet Hummus

Serves: 1

Cooking Time: 10 minutes

Ingredients:

- 5-6 large radishes, sliced
- 1/2 cup cooked beets, diced
- 1/2 cup chickpeas, rinsed and drained
- 1 tablespoon tahini
- 1 tablespoon lemon juice
- 1 clove garlic, minced
- 1 tablespoon olive oil
- Salt and pepper to taste

Instructions:

- In a blender or food processor, combine cooked beets, chickpeas, tahini, lemon juice, minced garlic, and olive oil.

- Blend until smooth. Season with salt and pepper to taste.
- Arrange radish slices on a plate.
- Serve the beet hummus alongside the radish slices.

Scientific Note:

- **Radishes**: Low in calories and high in fiber, providing essential vitamins and supporting digestion.
- **Beets**: Rich in antioxidants and nitrates, which can improve blood flow to the brain and support cognitive function.
- **Chickpeas**: Provide protein and fiber, which help maintain stable blood sugar levels and support cognitive function.
- **Tahini**: Made from sesame seeds, it is rich in healthy fats and magnesium, supporting brain health and cognitive function.
- **Garlic**: Known for its anti-inflammatory properties, which can help reduce inflammation in the brain.

Nutritional Information (Approximate):

- Calories: 220
- Protein: 6g
- Carbohydrates: 20g
- Fiber: 8g
- Sugars: 6g (Natural sugars from beets)
- Fat: 12g (Healthy fats)

Sweet Potato Chips with Avocado Dip

Serves: 1

Cooking Time: 25 minutes

Ingredients:

- 1 small sweet potato, thinly sliced
- 1/2 avocado
- 1 tablespoon lime juice
- 1 small garlic clove, minced
- 1 tablespoon chopped fresh cilantro
- 1 teaspoon olive oil
- Salt and pepper to taste

Instructions:

- Preheat the oven to 375°F (190°C).

- Toss sweet potato slices with olive oil, salt, and pepper. Arrange in a single layer on a baking sheet.
- Bake for 20 minutes or until crispy, flipping halfway through.
- In a small bowl, mash the avocado until smooth.
- Add lime juice, minced garlic, chopped cilantro, salt, and pepper to the mashed avocado. Mix well.
- Serve the sweet potato chips alongside the avocado dip.

Scientific Note:

- **Sweet potatoes:** High in fiber and vitamins, providing a steady release of energy and supporting cognitive function.
- **Avocado**: Contains healthy fats and folate, which support brain function and mood stabilization.
- **Lime juice**: High in vitamin C and antioxidants, supporting overall health.
- **Garlic**: Known for its anti-inflammatory properties, which can help reduce inflammation in the brain.
- **Cilantro**: Contains antioxidants and vitamins that support overall health.

Nutritional Information (Approximate):

- Calories: 250
- Protein: 3g
- Carbohydrates: 35g
- Fiber: 10g
- Sugars: 8g (Natural sugars from sweet potato)
- Fat: 14g (Healthy fats)

Zucchini Chips with Greek Yogurt Dill Dip

Serves: 1

Cooking Time: 20 minutes

Ingredients:

- 1 small zucchini, thinly sliced
- 1 tablespoon olive oil
- 1/4 teaspoon salt
- 1/4 teaspoon black pepper

For the Dip:

- 1/4 cup plain Greek yogurt
- 1 tablespoon fresh dill, chopped
- 1 teaspoon lemon juice
- 1 small garlic clove, minced
- Salt and pepper to taste

Instructions:

- Preheat the oven to 400°F (200°C).
- Toss zucchini slices with olive oil, salt, and pepper.
- Arrange the zucchini slices on a baking sheet in a single layer.
- Bake for 15-20 minutes until crispy, flipping halfway through.
- In a small bowl, combine Greek yogurt, chopped dill, lemon juice, minced garlic, salt, and pepper.
- Mix well and serve the dip alongside the zucchini chips.

Scientific Note:

- **Zucchini**: Low in calories and high in vitamins and minerals, supporting overall health and hydration.
- **Greek yogurt**: Rich in protein and probiotics, which can improve gut health and have a positive impact on brain function.
- **Dill**: Contains antioxidants and vitamins that support brain health.
- **Garlic**: Known for its anti-inflammatory properties, which can help reduce inflammation in the brain.

Nutritional Information (Approximate):

- Calories: 150
- Protein: 6g
- Carbohydrates: 10g
- Fiber: 2g
- Sugars: 4g (Natural sugars from yogurt)
- Fat: 10g (Healthy fats)

Cucumber Rounds with Spicy Chickpea Dip

Serves: 1

Cooking Time: 15 minutes

Ingredients:

- 1 small cucumber, sliced into rounds

- 1/2 cup cooked chickpeas
- 1 tablespoon tahini
- 1 tablespoon lemon juice
- 1 small garlic clove, minced
- 1/4 teaspoon cayenne pepper
- Salt and pepper to taste
- 1 tablespoon olive oil

Instructions:

- In a blender or food processor, combine cooked chickpeas, tahini, lemon juice, minced garlic, cayenne pepper, salt, pepper, and olive oil.
- Blend until smooth.
- Arrange cucumber rounds on a plate.
- Serve the spicy chickpea dip alongside the cucumber rounds.

Scientific Note:

- **Cucumber**: Provides hydration and antioxidants that support overall health and brain function.
- **Chickpeas**: Provide protein and fiber, which help maintain stable blood sugar levels and support cognitive function.
- **Tahini**: Made from sesame seeds, it is rich in healthy fats and magnesium, supporting brain health and cognitive function.
- **Cayenne pepper:** Contains capsaicin, which has antioxidant properties and can help boost metabolism.
- **Garlic**: Known for its anti-inflammatory properties, which can help reduce inflammation in the brain.

Nutritional Information (Approximate):

- Calories: 180
- Protein: 6g
- Carbohydrates: 15g
- Fiber: 5g
- Sugars: 4g (Natural sugars from cucumber)
- Fat: 10g (Healthy fats)

CHAPTER 5

SOUP AND STEW

Lentil and Spinach Soup

Serves: 1

Cooking Time: 30 minutes

Ingredients:

- 1/2 cup dried lentils, rinsed
- 1 cup fresh spinach leaves
- 1/2 carrot, diced
- 1/2 celery stalk, diced
- 1/2 small onion, diced
- 1 garlic clove, minced
- 2 cups low-sodium vegetable broth
- 1 tablespoon olive oil
- 1/2 teaspoon ground cumin
- 1/2 teaspoon turmeric
- Salt and pepper to taste
- Lemon wedge (for serving)

Instructions:

- In a large pot, heat olive oil over medium heat.
- Add diced onion, carrot, and celery. Sauté for about 5 minutes until vegetables are softened.
- Add minced garlic and cook for another minute.
- Stir in lentils, ground cumin, and turmeric. Cook for 1 minute to toast the spices.
- Add vegetable broth, bring to a boil, then reduce heat and simmer for 20 minutes, or until lentils are tender.
- Stir in fresh spinach and cook for another 2-3 minutes until wilted.
- Season with salt and pepper to taste.
- Serve with a lemon wedge on the side.

Scientific Note:

- **Lentils**: High in protein and fiber, lentils provide sustained energy and help maintain stable blood sugar levels.
- **Spinach**: Rich in iron, magnesium, and folate, spinach aids in brain health and reduces inflammation.

- **Carrot**: High in beta-carotene, which supports brain health and reduces inflammation.
- **Celery**: Contains antioxidants and vitamins that support overall health.
- **Turmeric**: Contains curcumin, which has anti-inflammatory properties and can enhance brain function.
- **Olive oil:** Contains monounsaturated fats and antioxidants that support brain health and reduce inflammation.

Nutritional Information (Approximate):

- Calories: 250
- Protein: 12g
- Carbohydrates: 35g
- Fiber: 12g
- Sugars: 6g (Natural sugars from vegetables)
- Fat: 8g (Healthy fats)

Butternut Squash and Chickpea Stew

Serves: 1

Cooking Time: 30 minutes

Ingredients:

- 1/2 small butternut squash, peeled and diced
- 1/2 cup cooked chickpeas
- 1/2 small onion, diced
- 1 garlic clove, minced
- 1 small tomato, diced
- 1 cup low-sodium vegetable broth
- 1 tablespoon olive oil
- 1/2 teaspoon ground cumin
- 1/2 teaspoon ground coriander
- 1/4 teaspoon ground cinnamon
- Salt and pepper to taste

- Fresh cilantro for garnish

Instructions:

- In a large pot, heat olive oil over medium heat.
- Add diced onion and sauté for about 5 minutes until softened.
- Add minced garlic and cook for another minute.
- Stir in diced butternut squash, chickpeas, ground cumin, ground coriander, and ground cinnamon. Cook for 2 minutes to toast the spices.
- Add diced tomato and vegetable broth. Bring to a boil, then reduce heat and simmer for 20 minutes, or until butternut squash is tender.
- Season with salt and pepper to taste.
- Garnish with fresh cilantro and serve immediately.

Scientific Note:

Butternut squash: Rich in vitamins A and C, which support brain health and reduce inflammation.

Chickpeas: Provide protein and fiber, which help maintain stable blood sugar levels and support cognitive function.

Tomato: Contains antioxidants such as lycopene, which support brain health.

Cumin and coriander: Contain antioxidants that support overall health and reduce inflammation.

Cinnamon: Contains antioxidants and helps stabilize blood sugar levels, which can prevent mood swings and hyperactivity.

Olive oil: Contains monounsaturated fats and antioxidants that support brain health and reduce inflammation.

Nutritional Information (Approximate):

- Calories: 280
- Protein: 8g
- Carbohydrates: 40g
- Fiber: 10g
- Sugars: 8g (Natural sugars from vegetables)
- Fat: 10g (Healthy fats)

Carrot Ginger Soup

Serves: 1

Cooking Time: 25 minutes

Ingredients:

- 2 large carrots, peeled and sliced
- 1/2 small onion, diced
- 1 small piece of ginger (about 1 inch), peeled and minced
- 1 clove garlic, minced
- 1 cup low-sodium vegetable broth
- 1/2 cup coconut milk (unsweetened)
- 1 tablespoon olive oil
- Salt and pepper to taste
- Fresh cilantro for garnish

Instructions:

- In a large pot, heat olive oil over medium heat.
- Add diced onion and sauté for about 5 minutes until softened.
- Add minced garlic and ginger, and cook for another minute.
- Add sliced carrots and vegetable broth. Bring to a boil, then reduce heat and simmer for 15 minutes until carrots are tender.
- Add coconut milk and cook for another 2 minutes.
- Blend the soup with an immersion blender or in a regular blender until smooth.
- Season with salt and pepper to taste.
- Garnish with fresh cilantro and serve immediately.

Scientific Note:

- **Carrots**: High in beta-carotene, which supports brain health and reduces inflammation.
- **Ginger**: Contains anti-inflammatory and antioxidant properties that support overall health and cognitive function.
- **Coconut milk**: Provides healthy fats that support brain function and reduce inflammation.

- **Garlic**: Known for its anti-inflammatory properties, which can help reduce inflammation in the brain.
- **Olive oil:** Contains monounsaturated fats and antioxidants that support brain health and reduce inflammation.

Nutritional Information (Approximate):

- Calories: 200
- Protein: 2g
- Carbohydrates: 20g
- Fiber: 5g
- Sugars: 10g (Natural sugars from carrots)
- Fat: 14g (Healthy fats)

Moroccan Lentil Stew

Serves: 1

Cooking Time: 30 minutes

Ingredients:

- 1/2 cup green lentils, rinsed
- 1/2 small onion, diced
- 1 small carrot, diced
- 1/2 zucchini, diced
- 1 clove garlic, minced
- 1 small tomato, diced
- 1 cup low-sodium vegetable broth
- 1 tablespoon olive oil
- 1/2 teaspoon ground cumin
- 1/2 teaspoon ground coriander
- 1/4 teaspoon ground cinnamon
- 1/4 teaspoon ground turmeric
- Salt and pepper to taste
- Fresh parsley for garnish

Instructions:

- In a large pot, heat olive oil over medium heat.
- Add diced onion and sauté for about 5 minutes until softened.
- Add minced garlic, ground cumin, ground coriander, ground cinnamon, and ground turmeric. Cook for another minute to toast the spices.
- Stir in diced carrot, zucchini, and tomato. Cook for 2-3 minutes.
- Add rinsed lentils and vegetable broth. Bring to a boil, then reduce heat and

- simmer for 20 minutes, or until lentils and vegetables are tender.
- Season with salt and pepper to taste.
- Garnish with fresh parsley and serve immediately.

Scientific Note:

- **Lentils**: High in protein and fiber, lentils provide sustained energy and help maintain stable blood sugar levels.
- **Carrot**: High in beta-carotene, which supports brain health and reduces inflammation.
- **Zucchini**: Low in calories and high in vitamins and minerals, supporting overall health.
- **Tomato**: Contains antioxidants such as lycopene, which support brain health.
- **Cumin and coriander**: Contain antioxidants that support overall health and reduce inflammation.
- **Turmeric**: Contains curcumin, which has anti-inflammatory properties and can enhance brain function.
- **Olive oil**: Contains monounsaturated fats and antioxidants that support brain health and reduce inflammation.

Nutritional Information (Approximate):

- Calories: 300
- Protein: 12g
- Carbohydrates: 40g
- Fiber: 12g
- Sugars: 8g (Natural sugars from vegetables)
- Fat: 10g (Healthy fats)

Sweet Potato and Red Lentil Soup

Serves: 1

Cooking Time: 30 minutes

Ingredients:

- 1 small sweet potato, peeled and diced
- 1/4 cup red lentils, rinsed
- 1/2 small onion, diced
- 1 small carrot, diced
- 1 clove garlic, minced
- 1/2 teaspoon ground cumin
- 1/2 teaspoon ground ginger

- 1 cup low-sodium vegetable broth
- 1 tablespoon olive oil
- Salt and pepper to taste
- Fresh cilantro for garnish

Instructions:

- In a large pot, heat olive oil over medium heat.
- Add diced onion and carrot, and sauté for about 5 minutes until softened.
- Add minced garlic, ground cumin, and ground ginger, and cook for another minute.
- Add diced sweet potato, red lentils, and vegetable broth.
- Bring to a boil, then reduce heat and simmer for 20 minutes, or until sweet potato and lentils are tender.
- Blend the soup with an immersion blender or in a regular blender until smooth.
- Season with salt and pepper to taste.
- Garnish with fresh cilantro and serve immediately.

Scientific Note:

- Sweet potato: High in fiber and vitamins, providing a steady release of energy and supporting cognitive function.
- Red lentils: High in protein and fiber, helping to maintain stable blood sugar levels and supporting cognitive function.
- Ginger: Contains anti-inflammatory and antioxidant properties that support overall health and cognitive function.
- Cumin: Contains antioxidants that support overall health and reduce inflammation.
- Olive oil: Contains monounsaturated fats and antioxidants that support brain health and reduce inflammation.

Nutritional Information (Approximate):

- Calories: 250
- Protein: 8g
- Carbohydrates: 40g
- Fiber: 10g
- Sugars: 10g (Natural sugars from sweet potato)
- Fat: 8g (Healthy fats)

Chickpea and Kale Stew

Serves: 1

Cooking Time: 30 minutes

Ingredients:

- 1/2 cup cooked chickpeas
- 1 cup chopped kale
- 1/2 small onion, diced
- 1 small tomato, diced
- 1 small carrot, diced
- 1 clove garlic, minced
- 1 teaspoon ground turmeric
- 1 teaspoon ground cumin
- 1 cup low-sodium vegetable broth
- 1 tablespoon olive oil
- Salt and pepper to taste
- Fresh parsley for garnish

Instructions:

- In a large pot, heat olive oil over medium heat.
- Add diced onion and carrot, and sauté for about 5 minutes until softened.
- Add minced garlic, ground turmeric, and ground cumin, and cook for another minute.
- Add cooked chickpeas, chopped kale, diced tomato, and vegetable broth.
- Bring to a boil, then reduce heat and simmer for 20 minutes, or until vegetables are tender.
- Season with salt and pepper to taste.
- Garnish with fresh parsley and serve immediately.

Scientific Note:

- **Chickpeas**: Provide protein and fiber, helping to maintain stable blood sugar levels and supporting cognitive function.
- **Kale**: Rich in vitamins and antioxidants, supporting brain health and reducing inflammation.
- **Tomato**: Contains antioxidants such as lycopene, which support brain health.
- **Turmeric**: Contains curcumin, which has anti-inflammatory properties and can enhance brain function.

- **Cumin**: Contains antioxidants that support overall health and reduce inflammation.
- **Olive oil:** Contains monounsaturated fats and antioxidants that support brain health and reduce inflammation.

Nutritional Information (Approximate):

- Calories: 280
- Protein: 10g
- Carbohydrates: 35g
- Fiber: 12g
- Sugars: 8g (Natural sugars from vegetables)
- Fat: 10g (Healthy fats)

Green Pea and Mint Soup

Serves: 1

Cooking Time: 20 minutes

Ingredients:

- 1 cup green peas (fresh or frozen)
- 1/4 small onion, diced
- 1 small potato, peeled and diced
- 1 garlic clove, minced
- 1 cup low-sodium vegetable broth
- 1/4 cup fresh mint leaves
- 1 tablespoon olive oil
- Salt and pepper to taste
- Lemon wedge (for serving)

Instructions:

- In a large pot, heat olive oil over medium heat.
- Add diced onion and sauté for about 5 minutes until softened.
- Add minced garlic and cook for another minute.
- Add diced potato and vegetable broth. Bring to a boil, then reduce heat and simmer for 10 minutes until potato is tender.
- Add green peas and cook for another 5 minutes.
- Stir in fresh mint leaves.
- Blend the soup with an immersion blender or in a regular blender until smooth.
- Season with salt and pepper to taste.
- Serve with a lemon wedge.

Scientific Note:

- **Green peas:** High in protein, fiber, and vitamins, which support cognitive function and provide steady energy.
- **Potato**: Provides complex carbohydrates and fiber for sustained energy release.
- **Mint**: Contains antioxidants and essential oils that support overall health.
- **Olive oil**: Contains monounsaturated fats and antioxidants that support brain health and reduce inflammation.

Nutritional Information (Approximate):

- Calories: 180
- Protein: 6g
- Carbohydrates: 30g
- Fiber: 8g
- Sugars: 6g (Natural sugars from vegetables)
- Fat: 7g (Healthy fat

Eggplant and Tomato Stew

Serves: 1

Cooking Time: 30 minutes

Ingredients:

- 1/2 medium eggplant, diced
- 1 small tomato, diced
- 1/4 small onion, diced
- 1 garlic clove, minced
- 1/4 red bell pepper, diced
- 1/2 teaspoon ground cumin
- 1/2 teaspoon smoked paprika
- 1 cup low-sodium vegetable broth
- 1 tablespoon olive oil
- Salt and pepper to taste
- Fresh basil for garnish

Instructions:

- In a large pot, heat olive oil over medium heat.
- Add diced onion and red bell pepper, and sauté for about 5 minutes until softened.
- Add minced garlic, ground cumin, and smoked paprika, and cook for another minute.
- Add diced eggplant, tomato, and vegetable broth.
- Bring to a boil, then reduce heat and simmer for 20 minutes, or until eggplant is tender.
- Season with salt and pepper to taste.
- Garnish with fresh basil and serve immediately.

Scientific Note:

- **Eggplant**: Rich in antioxidants and fiber, supporting brain health and reducing inflammation.
- **Tomato**: Contains antioxidants such as lycopene, which support brain health.
- **Red bell pepper**: High in vitamin C and antioxidants, supporting cognitive function.
- **Cumin and smoked paprika**: Contain antioxidants that support overall health and reduce inflammation.
- **Olive oil:** Contains monounsaturated fats and antioxidants that support brain health and reduce inflammation.

Nutritional Information (Approximate):

- Calories: 200
- Protein: 4g
- Carbohydrates: 30g
- Fiber: 8g
- Sugars: 10g (Natural sugars from vegetables)
- Fat: 9g (Healthy fats)

Broccoli and Cauliflower Soup

Serves: 1

Cooking Time: 25 minutes

Ingredients:

- 1 cup broccoli florets
- 1 cup cauliflower florets
- 1/4 small onion, diced
- 1 clove garlic, minced
- 1 cup low-sodium vegetable broth
- 1/2 cup unsweetened almond milk
- 1 tablespoon olive oil
- Salt and pepper to taste
- Fresh chives for garnish

Instructions:

- In a large pot, heat olive oil over medium heat.
- Add diced onion and sauté for about 5 minutes until softened.
- Add minced garlic and cook for another minute.
- Add broccoli, cauliflower, and vegetable broth. Bring to a boil, then reduce heat and simmer for 15 minutes until vegetables are tender.
- Add almond milk and cook for another 2 minutes.
- Blend the soup with an immersion blender or in a regular blender until smooth.
- Season with salt and pepper to taste.
- Garnish with fresh chives and serve immediately.

Scientific Note:

- Broccoli: Rich in vitamins C and K, and antioxidants that support brain health and reduce inflammation.
- Cauliflower: High in fiber and antioxidants, supporting overall health and cognitive function.
- Almond milk: Provides healthy fats and vitamin E, supporting brain health.
- Olive oil: Contains monounsaturated fats and antioxidants that support brain health and reduce inflammation.

Nutritional Information (Approximate):

- Calories: 180
- Protein: 6g
- Carbohydrates: 18g
- Fiber: 6g
- Sugars: 4g (Natural sugars from vegetables)
- Fat: 10g (Healthy fats)

White Bean and Kale Stew

Serves: 1

Cooking Time: 30 minutes

Ingredients:

- 1/2 cup cooked white beans
- 1 cup chopped kale
- 1/2 small onion, diced
- 1 small carrot, diced
- 1 clove garlic, minced
- 1 small tomato, diced
- 1 cup low-sodium vegetable broth
- 1 tablespoon olive oil
- 1/2 teaspoon dried thyme
- 1/2 teaspoon dried oregano
- Salt and pepper to taste
- Fresh parsley for garnish

Instructions:

- In a large pot, heat olive oil over medium heat.
- Add diced onion and carrot, and sauté for about 5 minutes until softened.
- Add minced garlic, dried thyme, and dried oregano, and cook for another minute.
- Add cooked white beans, chopped kale, diced tomato, and vegetable broth.
- Bring to a boil, then reduce heat and simmer for 20 minutes, or until vegetables are tender.
- Season with salt and pepper to taste.
- Garnish with fresh parsley and serve immediately.

Scientific Note:

- White beans: High in protein and fiber, providing sustained energy and supporting cognitive function.
- Kale: Rich in vitamins and antioxidants, supporting brain health and reducing inflammation.
- Tomato: Contains antioxidants such as lycopene, which support brain health.
- Thyme and oregano: Contain antioxidants that support overall health and reduce inflammation.
- Olive oil: Contains monounsaturated fats and antioxidants that support brain health and reduce inflammation.

Nutritional Information (Approximate):

- Calories: 220
- Protein: 10g
- Carbohydrates: 28g
- Fiber: 10g
- Sugars: 6g (Natural sugars from vegetables)
- Fat: 8g (Healthy fats)

CHAPTER 6

DINNER RECIPES

Quinoa-Stuffed Bell Peppers

Serves: 1

Cooking Time: 40 minutes

Ingredients:

- 1 large bell pepper
- 1/2 cup cooked quinoa
- 1/4 cup black beans, rinsed and drained
- 1/4 cup corn kernels (fresh or frozen)
- 1/4 small onion, diced
- 1 clove garlic, minced
- 1/4 cup diced tomatoes
- 1 tablespoon olive oil
- 1/2 teaspoon ground cumin

- 1/2 teaspoon smoked paprika
- Salt and pepper to taste
- Fresh cilantro for garnish

Instructions:

- Preheat the oven to 375°F (190°C).
- Cut the top off the bell pepper and remove the seeds and membranes.
- In a skillet, heat olive oil over medium heat.
- Add diced onion and sauté for about 5 minutes until softened.
- Add minced garlic, ground cumin, and smoked paprika, and cook for another minute.
- Stir in cooked quinoa, black beans, corn, and diced tomatoes. Cook for 2-3 minutes until heated through.
- Season with salt and pepper to taste.
- Stuff the bell pepper with the quinoa mixture and place it in a baking dish.
- Bake for 25-30 minutes until the pepper is tender.
- Garnish with fresh cilantro and serve immediately.

Scientific Note:

- **Quinoa**: High in protein and fiber, providing steady energy and supporting cognitive function.
- **Black beans:** Provide protein and fiber, helping to maintain stable blood sugar levels and support cognitive function.
- **Bell pepper:** Rich in vitamin C and antioxidants, supporting cognitive function and reducing inflammation.
- **Corn**: Provides vitamins and minerals that support overall health.
- **Olive oil:** Contains monounsaturated fats and antioxidants that support brain health and reduce inflammation.

Nutritional Information (Approximate):

- Calories: 350
- Protein: 12g
- Carbohydrates: 55g
- Fiber: 10g
- Sugars: 10g (Natural sugars from vegetables)
- Fat: 12g (Healthy fats)

Baked Salmon with Asparagus and Sweet Potato

Serves: 1

Cooking Time: 30 minutes

Ingredients:

- 1 salmon fillet (about 6 oz)
- 1 small sweet potato, peeled and diced
- 1 cup asparagus, trimmed
- 1 tablespoon olive oil
- 1 teaspoon lemon juice
- 1 clove garlic, minced
- Salt and pepper to taste
- Fresh parsley for garnish

Instructions:

- Preheat the oven to 400°F (200°C).
- In a baking dish, toss diced sweet potato with 1/2 tablespoon olive oil, minced garlic, salt, and pepper. Spread in a single layer and bake for 10 minutes.
- Remove the baking dish from the oven and add the salmon fillet and asparagus.
- Drizzle the salmon and asparagus with the remaining olive oil and lemon juice. Season with salt and pepper.
- Return the baking dish to the oven and bake for an additional 15-20 minutes until the salmon is cooked through and the sweet potato is tender.
- Garnish with fresh parsley and serve immediately.

Scientific Note:

- **Salmon**: Rich in omega-3 fatty acids, which are essential for brain health and can help manage ADHD symptoms.
- **Sweet potato**: High in fiber and vitamins, providing a steady release of energy and supporting cognitive function.
- **Asparagus**: Rich in vitamins A, C, and K, and antioxidants that support brain health and reduce inflammation.
- **Olive oil**: Contains monounsaturated fats and antioxidants that support brain health and reduce inflammation.
- **Garlic**: Known for its anti-inflammatory properties, which can help reduce inflammation in the brain.

Nutritional Information (Approximate):

- Calories: 450
- Protein: 30g
- Carbohydrates: 35g
- Fiber: 8g
- Sugars: 8g (Natural sugars from vegetables)
- Fat: 22g (Healthy fats)

Stuffed Portobello Mushrooms

Serves: 1

Cooking Time: 25 minutes

Ingredients:

- 2 large Portobello mushrooms, stems removed
- 1/2 cup cooked wild rice
- 1/4 cup cherry tomatoes, diced
- 1/4 cup chopped spinach
- 1/4 small red onion, diced
- 1 clove garlic, minced
- 1 tablespoon pine nuts
- 1 tablespoon olive oil
- 1/2 teaspoon dried thyme
- Salt and pepper to taste
- Fresh basil for garnish

Instructions:

- Preheat the oven to 375°F (190°C).
- In a skillet, heat olive oil over medium heat.
- Add diced red onion and sauté for about 5 minutes until softened.
- Add minced garlic and cook for another minute.
- Stir in cooked wild rice, diced cherry tomatoes, chopped spinach, pine nuts, dried thyme, salt, and pepper. Cook for 2-3 minutes until heated through.
- Place the Portobello mushrooms on a baking sheet and fill them with the rice mixture.
- Bake for 15-20 minutes until the mushrooms are tender.
- Garnish with fresh basil and serve immediately.

Scientific Note:

- **Portobello mushrooms**: Rich in B vitamins and antioxidants, supporting brain health and reducing inflammation.
- **Wild rice**: High in protein and fiber, providing steady energy and supporting cognitive function.
- **Spinach**: Rich in iron, magnesium, and folate, aiding in brain health and reducing inflammation.
- **Pine nuts**: Provide healthy fats and magnesium, which support brain health.
- **Olive oil:** Contains monounsaturated fats and antioxidants that support brain health and reduce inflammation.

Nutritional Information (Approximate):

- Calories: 300
- Protein: 10g
- Carbohydrates: 40g
- Fiber: 8g
- Sugars: 6g (Natural sugars from vegetables)
- Fat: 12g (Healthy fats)

Grilled Chicken with Quinoa and Roasted Vegetables

Serves: 1

Cooking Time: 35 minutes

Ingredients:

- 1 boneless, skinless chicken breast
- 1/2 cup cooked quinoa
- 1/2 zucchini, sliced
- 1/2 red bell pepper, sliced
- 1/4 red onion, sliced
- 1 tablespoon olive oil
- 1 teaspoon dried oregano
- 1 clove garlic, minced
- Salt and pepper to taste
- Fresh parsley for garnish

Instructions:

- Preheat the oven to 400°F (200°C).
- In a baking dish, toss sliced zucchini, red bell pepper, and red onion with olive oil, minced garlic, dried oregano, salt, and pepper.
- Spread the vegetables in a single layer and roast for 20-25 minutes until tender.
- While the vegetables are roasting, season the chicken breast with salt and pepper.
- Heat a grill pan over medium-high heat and cook the chicken for about 6-7 minutes on each side until fully cooked.
- Serve the grilled chicken with cooked quinoa and roasted vegetables.
- Garnish with fresh parsley and serve immediately.

Scientific Note:

- Chicken breast: A good source of lean protein, essential for maintaining muscle mass and energy levels, contributing to better focus.
- Quinoa: High in protein and fiber, providing steady energy and supporting cognitive function.
- Zucchini: Low in calories and high in vitamins and minerals, supporting overall health.
- Red bell pepper: Rich in vitamin C and antioxidants, supporting cognitive function and reducing inflammation.
- Olive oil: Contains monounsaturated fats and antioxidants that support brain health and reduce inflammation.

Nutritional Information (Approximate):

- Calories: 450
- Protein: 30g
- Carbohydrates: 40g
- Fiber: 8g
- Sugars: 10g (Natural sugars from vegetables)
- Fat: 16g (Healthy fats)

Baked Cod with Herb Quinoa and Steamed Broccoli

Serves: 1

Cooking Time: 30 minutes

Ingredients:

- 1 cod fillet (about 6 oz)
- 1/2 cup cooked quinoa
- 1 cup broccoli florets
- 1 tablespoon olive oil
- 1 tablespoon lemon juice
- 1 garlic clove, minced
- 1 teaspoon dried dill
- 1 teaspoon dried parsley
- Salt and pepper to taste
- Fresh lemon slices for garnish

Instructions:

- Preheat the oven to 375°F (190°C).
- Place the cod fillet on a baking sheet lined with parchment paper. Drizzle with half of the olive oil and lemon juice. Season with salt, pepper, minced garlic, and dried dill.
- Bake the cod for 15-20 minutes, or until the fish is opaque and flakes easily with a fork.
- While the cod is baking, steam the broccoli florets until tender, about 5-7 minutes.
- In a small pot, combine cooked quinoa, the remaining olive oil, dried parsley, salt, and pepper. Stir to combine and heat through.
- Serve the baked cod with herb quinoa and steamed broccoli. Garnish with fresh lemon slices.

Scientific Note:

- **Cod**: A lean source of protein and omega-3 fatty acids, supporting brain health and cognitive function.
- **Quinoa**: High in protein and fiber, providing steady energy and supporting cognitive function.
- **Broccoli**: Rich in vitamins C and K, and antioxidants that support brain health and reduce inflammation.

- **Olive oil**: Contains monounsaturated fats and antioxidants that support brain health and reduce inflammation.

Nutritional Information (Approximate):

- Calories: 350
- Protein: 30g
- Carbohydrates: 32g
- Fiber: 6g
- Sugars: 2g (Natural sugars from vegetables)
- Fat: 12g (Healthy fats)

Turkey and Vegetable Stir-Fry

Serves: 1

Cooking Time: 25 minutes

Ingredients:

- 1/2 pound ground turkey
- 1/2 cup snap peas
- 1/2 red bell pepper, sliced
- 1/2 zucchini, sliced
- 1/4 cup shredded carrots
- 1 small onion, diced
- 2 tablespoons coconut aminos (soy-free alternative)
- 1 tablespoon olive oil
- 1 garlic clove, minced
- 1 teaspoon grated fresh ginger
- Salt and pepper to taste
- Fresh cilantro for garnish

Instructions:

- In a large skillet, heat olive oil over medium heat.
- Add diced onion and sauté for about 5 minutes until softened.
- Add minced garlic and grated ginger, and cook for another minute.
- Add ground turkey and cook until browned and fully cooked, about 7-10 minutes.
- Add snap peas, red bell pepper, zucchini, and shredded carrots. Cook for 5-7 minutes until vegetables are tender-crisp.
- Stir in coconut aminos and cook for another 2 minutes.
- Season with salt and pepper to taste.

- Garnish with fresh cilantro and serve immediately.

Scientific Note:

- **Turkey**: A lean source of protein, essential for maintaining muscle mass and energy levels, contributing to better focus.
- **Snap peas:** Provide fiber and vitamins that support overall health.
- **Red bell pepper**: Rich in vitamin C and antioxidants, supporting cognitive function and reducing inflammation.
- **Zucchini**: Low in calories and high in vitamins and minerals, supporting overall health.
- **Carrots**: High in beta-carotene, which supports brain health and reduces inflammation.
- **Olive oil:** Contains monounsaturated fats and antioxidants that support brain health and reduce inflammation.
- **Ginger**: Contains anti-inflammatory and antioxidant properties that support overall health and cognitive function.

Nutritional Information (Approximate):

- Calories: 400
- Protein: 35g
- Carbohydrates: 20g
- Fiber: 6g
- Sugars: 8g (Natural sugars from vegetables)
- Fat: 20g (Healthy fats)

Grilled Shrimp with Avocado and Mango Salad

Serves: 1

Cooking Time: 20 minutes

Ingredients:

- 6 large shrimp, peeled and deveined
- 1/2 avocado, diced
- 1/2 mango, diced
- 1/4 red onion, finely chopped
- 1 tablespoon lime juice
- 1 tablespoon olive oil
- Salt and pepper to taste
- Fresh cilantro for garnish

Instructions:

- Preheat the grill to medium-high heat.
- In a bowl, toss the shrimp with half of the lime juice, olive oil, salt, and pepper.
- Grill the shrimp for about 2-3 minutes on each side until pink and cooked through.
- In another bowl, combine diced avocado, mango, red onion, and the remaining lime juice.
- Season the avocado and mango salad with salt and pepper to taste.
- Serve the grilled shrimp on top of the avocado and mango salad.
- Garnish with fresh cilantro and serve immediately.

Scientific Note:

- **Shrimp**: High in protein and omega-3 fatty acids, supporting brain health and cognitive function.
- **Avocado**: Contains healthy fats and folate, supporting brain function and mood stabilization.
- **Mango**: Rich in vitamins A and C, which support immune function and overall health.
- **Red onion:** Contains antioxidants and vitamins that support brain health.
- **Olive oil:** Contains monounsaturated fats and antioxidants that support brain health and reduce inflammation.

Nutritional Information (Approximate):

- Calories: 350
- Protein: 25g
- Carbohydrates: 20g
- Fiber: 8g
- Sugars: 10g (Natural sugars from mango)
- Fat: 18g (Healthy fats)

Lentil and Spinach Curry

Serves: 1

Cooking Time: 30 minutes

Ingredients:

- 1/2 cup dried lentils, rinsed
- 1 cup fresh spinach leaves
- 1/2 small tomato, diced
- 1/4 small onion, diced
- 1 clove garlic, minced
- 1/2 teaspoon grated fresh ginger

- 1 teaspoon curry powder
- 1/2 teaspoon ground cumin
- 1 cup low-sodium vegetable broth
- 1 tablespoon coconut oil
- Salt and pepper to taste
- Fresh cilantro for garnish

Instructions:

- In a large pot, heat coconut oil over medium heat.
- Add diced onion and sauté for about 5 minutes until softened.
- Add minced garlic, grated ginger, curry powder, and ground cumin, and cook for another minute.
- Stir in rinsed lentils and vegetable broth. Bring to a boil, then reduce heat and simmer for 20 minutes, or until lentils are tender.
- Add diced tomato and fresh spinach leaves. Cook until the spinach is wilted, about 2-3 minutes.
- Season with salt and pepper to taste.
- Garnish with fresh cilantro and serve immediately.

Scientific Note:

- **Lentils**: High in protein and fiber, providing sustained energy and supporting cognitive function.
- **Spinach**: Rich in iron, magnesium, and folate, aiding in brain health and reducing inflammation.
- **Tomato**: Contains antioxidants such as lycopene, which support brain health.
- **Coconut oil:** Provides medium-chain triglycerides (MCTs), which are beneficial fats that support brain function.
- **Ginger**: Contains anti-inflammatory and antioxidant properties that support overall health and cognitive function.

Nutritional Information (Approximate):

- Calories: 320
- Protein: 15g
- Carbohydrates: 40g
- Fiber: 15g
- Sugars: 8g (Natural sugars from vegetables)
- Fat: 12g (Healthy fats)

Grilled Eggplant with Chickpea and Tomato Salad

Serves: 1

Cooking Time: 25 minutes

Ingredients:

- 1 small eggplant, sliced into rounds
- 1/2 cup cooked chickpeas
- 1/2 cup cherry tomatoes, halved
- 1/4 small red onion, finely chopped
- 1 tablespoon fresh parsley, chopped
- 1 tablespoon olive oil
- 1 tablespoon lemon juice
- 1 clove garlic, minced
- Salt and pepper to taste

Instructions:

- Preheat the grill to medium-high heat.
- Brush the eggplant slices with olive oil and season with salt and pepper.
- Grill the eggplant slices for about 3-4 minutes on each side until tender and charred.
- In a bowl, combine cooked chickpeas, cherry tomatoes, red onion, fresh parsley, lemon juice, and minced garlic. Toss to combine.
- Season the salad with salt and pepper to taste.
- Serve the grilled eggplant slices topped with the chickpea and tomato salad.

Scientific Note:

- **Eggplant**: Rich in antioxidants and fiber, supporting brain health and reducing inflammation.
- **Chickpeas**: High in protein and fiber, providing sustained energy and supporting cognitive function.
- **Cherry tomatoes**: Contain antioxidants such as lycopene, which support brain health.
- **Red onion**: Provides antioxidants and vitamins that support brain health.
- **Olive oil:** Contains monounsaturated fats and antioxidants that support brain health and reduce inflammation.

Nutritional Information (Approximate):

- Calories: 320
- Protein: 10g
- Carbohydrates: 35g
- Fiber: 10g
- Sugars: 8g (Natural sugars from vegetables)
- Fat: 16g (Healthy fats)

Turkey Meatballs with Zucchini Noodles

Serves: 1

Cooking Time: 30 minutes

Ingredients:

- 1/4 pound ground turkey
- 1 small zucchini, spiralized into noodles
- 1/4 small onion, finely chopped
- 1 clove garlic, minced
- 1 tablespoon fresh basil, chopped
- 1/2 teaspoon dried oregano
- 1/4 cup crushed tomatoes (no added sugar)
- 1 tablespoon olive oil
- Salt and pepper to taste
- Fresh parsley for garnish

Instructions:

- In a bowl, combine ground turkey, chopped onion, minced garlic, fresh basil, dried oregano, salt, and pepper. Mix well and form into small meatballs.
- Heat olive oil in a skillet over medium heat. Add the meatballs and cook for about 8-10 minutes, turning occasionally, until browned and cooked through.
- Remove the meatballs from the skillet and set aside.
- In the same skillet, add crushed tomatoes and cook for 2-3 minutes until heated through.
- Add the zucchini noodles to the skillet and cook for 2-3 minutes until tender.
- Return the meatballs to the skillet and toss with the sauce and zucchini noodles.
- Garnish with fresh parsley and serve immediately.

Scientific Note:

- **Ground turkey**: A lean source of protein, essential for maintaining muscle mass and energy levels, contributing to better focus.
- **Zucchini:** Low in calories and high in vitamins and minerals, supporting overall health.
- **Crushed tomatoes:** Contain antioxidants such as lycopene, which support brain health.
- **Garlic:** Known for its anti-inflammatory properties, which can help reduce inflammation in the brain.
- **Olive oil:** Contains monounsaturated fats and antioxidants that support brain health and reduce inflammation.

Nutritional Information (Approximate):

- Calories: 350
- Protein: 25g
- Carbohydrates: 20g
- Fiber: 5g
- Sugars: 8g (Natural sugars from vegetables)
- Fat: 18g (Healthy fats)

CHAPTER 7
30 DAYS MEAL PLAN
Week 1

Day 1

Breakfast: Avocado and Egg Toast

Lunch: Grilled Chicken and Quinoa Salad

Snack: Carrot Sticks with Tahini Dip

Soup: Lentil and Spinach Soup

Dinner: Quinoa-Stuffed Bell Peppers

Day 2

Breakfast: Banana and Almond Butter Smoothie

Lunch: Lentil and Vegetable Stir-Fry

Snack: Cucumber Slices with Avocado Dip

Stew: Butternut Squash and Chickpea Stew

Dinner: Baked Salmon with Asparagus and Sweet Potato

Day 3

Breakfast: Greek Yogurt Parfait

Lunch: Turkey and Avocado Lettuce Wraps

Snack: Celery Sticks with Almond Butter Dip

Soup: Carrot Ginger Soup

Dinner: Stuffed Portobello Mushrooms

Day 4

Breakfast: Sweet Potato and Spinach Hash

Lunch: Salmon and Quinoa Stuffed Peppers

Snack: Bell Pepper Strips with Hummus

Stew: Moroccan Lentil Stew

Dinner: Grilled Chicken with Quinoa and Roasted Vegetables

Day 5

Breakfast: Quinoa Breakfast Bowl

Lunch: Chickpea and Spinach Salad

Snack: Apple Slices with Sunflower Seed Butter Dip

Soup: Sweet Potato and Red Lentil Soup

Dinner: Baked Cod with Herb Quinoa and Steamed Broccoli

Day 6

Breakfast: Veggie Omelette with Goat Cheese

Lunch: Lentil and Vegetable Soup

Snack: Jicama Sticks with Guacamole

Stew: Chickpea and Kale Stew

Dinner: Turkey and Vegetable Stir-Fry

Day 7

Breakfast: Chickpea Pancakes with Spinach and Tomato

Lunch: Butternut Squash and Black Bean Tacos

Snack: Radish Slices with Beet Hummus

Soup: Green Pea and Mint Soup

Dinner: Grilled Shrimp with Avocado and Mango Salad

Week 2

Day 8

Breakfast: Baked Sweet Potato and Black Bean Hash

Lunch: Quinoa and Edamame Salad

Snack: Sweet Potato Chips with Avocado Dip

Stew: Eggplant and Tomato Stew

Dinner: Lentil and Spinach Curry

Day 9

Breakfast: Smoked Salmon and Avocado Wrap

Lunch: Grilled Portobello Mushroom and Quinoa Bowl

Snack: Zucchini Chips with Greek Yogurt Dill Dip

Soup: Broccoli and Cauliflower Soup

Dinner: Grilled Eggplant with Chickpea and Tomato Salad

Day 10

Breakfast: Apple Cinnamon Quinoa Porridge

Lunch: Zucchini Noodles with Pesto and Grilled Shrimp

Snack: Cucumber Rounds with Spicy Chickpea Dip

Stew: White Bean and Kale Stew

Dinner: Turkey Meatballs with Zucchini Noodles

Day 11

Breakfast: Avocado and Egg Toast

Lunch: Grilled Chicken and Quinoa Salad

Snack: Carrot Sticks with Tahini Dip

Soup: Lentil and Spinach Soup

Dinner: Quinoa-Stuffed Bell Peppers

Day 12

Breakfast: Banana and Almond Butter Smoothie

Lunch: Lentil and Vegetable Stir-Fry

Snack: Cucumber Slices with Avocado Dip

Stew: Butternut Squash and Chickpea Stew

Dinner: Baked Salmon with Asparagus and Sweet Potato

Day 13

Breakfast: Greek Yogurt Parfait

Lunch: Turkey and Avocado Lettuce Wraps

Snack: Celery Sticks with Almond Butter Dip

Soup: Carrot Ginger Soup

Dinner: Stuffed Portobello Mushrooms

Day 14

Breakfast: Sweet Potato and Spinach Hash

Lunch: Salmon and Quinoa Stuffed Peppers

Snack: Bell Pepper Strips with Hummus

Stew: Moroccan Lentil Stew

Dinner: Grilled Chicken with Quinoa and Roasted Vegetables

Week 3

Day 15

Breakfast: Quinoa Breakfast Bowl

Lunch: Chickpea and Spinach Salad

Snack: Apple Slices with Sunflower Seed Butter Dip

Soup: Sweet Potato and Red Lentil Soup

Dinner: Baked Cod with Herb Quinoa and Steamed Broccoli

Day 16

Breakfast: Veggie Omelette with Goat Cheese

Lunch: Lentil and Vegetable Soup

Snack: Jicama Sticks with Guacamole

Stew: Chickpea and Kale Stew

Dinner: Turkey and Vegetable Stir-Fry

Day 17

Breakfast: Chickpea Pancakes with Spinach and Tomato

Lunch: Butternut Squash and Black Bean Tacos

Snack: Radish Slices with Beet Hummus

Soup: Green Pea and Mint Soup

Dinner: Grilled Shrimp with Avocado and Mango Salad

Day 18

Breakfast: Baked Sweet Potato and Black Bean Hash

Lunch: Quinoa and Edamame Salad

Snack: Sweet Potato Chips with Avocado Dip

Stew: Eggplant and Tomato Stew

Dinner: Lentil and Spinach Curry

Day 19

Breakfast: Smoked Salmon and Avocado Wrap

Lunch: Grilled Portobello Mushroom and Quinoa Bowl

Snack: Zucchini Chips with Greek Yogurt Dill Dip

Soup: Broccoli and Cauliflower Soup

Dinner: Grilled Eggplant with Chickpea and Tomato Salad

Day 20

Breakfast: Apple Cinnamon Quinoa Porridge

Lunch: Zucchini Noodles with Pesto and Grilled Shrimp

Snack: Cucumber Rounds with Spicy Chickpea Dip

Stew: White Bean and Kale Stew

Dinner: Turkey Meatballs with Zucchini Noodles

Day 21

Breakfast: Avocado and Egg Toast

Lunch: Grilled Chicken and Quinoa Salad

Snack: Carrot Sticks with Tahini Dip

Soup: Lentil and Spinach Soup

Dinner: Quinoa-Stuffed Bell Peppers

Week 4

Day 22

Breakfast: Banana and Almond Butter Smoothie

Lunch: Lentil and Vegetable Stir-Fry

Snack: Cucumber Slices with Avocado Dip

Stew: Butternut Squash and Chickpea Stew

Dinner: Baked Salmon with Asparagus and Sweet Potato

Day 23

Breakfast: Greek Yogurt Parfait

Lunch: Turkey and Avocado Lettuce Wraps

Snack: Celery Sticks with Almond Butter Dip

Soup: Carrot Ginger Soup

Dinner: Stuffed Portobello Mushrooms

Day 24

Breakfast: Sweet Potato and Spinach Hash

Lunch: Salmon and Quinoa Stuffed Peppers

Snack: Bell Pepper Strips with Hummus

Stew: Moroccan Lentil Stew

Dinner: Grilled Chicken with Quinoa and Roasted Vegetables

Day 25

Breakfast: Quinoa Breakfast Bowl

Lunch: Chickpea and Spinach Salad

Snack: Apple Slices with Sunflower Seed Butter Dip

Soup: Sweet Potato and Red Lentil Soup

Dinner: Baked Cod with Herb Quinoa and Steamed Broccoli

Day 26

Breakfast: Veggie Omelette with Goat Cheese

Lunch: Lentil and Vegetable Soup

Snack: Jicama Sticks with Guacamole

Stew: Chickpea and Kale Stew

Dinner: Turkey and Vegetable Stir-Fry

Day 27

Breakfast: Chickpea Pancakes with Spinach and Tomato

Lunch: Butternut Squash and Black Bean Tacos

Snack: Radish Slices with Beet Hummus

Soup: Green Pea and Mint Soup

Dinner: Grilled Shrimp with Avocado and Mango Salad

Day 28

Breakfast: Baked Sweet Potato and Black Bean Hash

Lunch: Quinoa and Edamame Salad

Snack: Sweet Potato Chips with Avocado Dip

Stew: Eggplant and Tomato Stew

Dinner: Lentil and Spinach Curry

Day 29

Breakfast: Smoked Salmon and Avocado Wrap

Lunch: Grilled Portobello Mushroom and Quinoa Bowl

Snack: Zucchini Chips with Greek Yogurt Dill Dip

Soup: Broccoli and Cauliflower Soup

Dinner: Grilled Eggplant with Chickpea and Tomato Salad

Day 30

Breakfast: Apple Cinnamon Quinoa Porridge

Lunch: Zucchini Noodles with Pesto and Grilled Shrimp

Snack: Cucumber Rounds with Spicy Chickpea Dip

Stew: White Bean and Kale Stew

Dinner: Turkey Meatballs with Zucchini Noodles

SCIENTIFIC RECOMMENDATION: ADHD-FRIENDLY SHOPPING LIST

Produce

- Avocado (4)
- Bananas (3)
- Blueberries (1 cup)
- Carrots (6)
- Celery (4 stalks)
- Cherry tomatoes (1 pint)
- Cucumber (3)
- Fresh cilantro (1 bunch)
- Fresh dill (1 bunch)
- Fresh ginger (1 small piece)
- Fresh mint (1 bunch)
- Fresh parsley (1 bunch)
- Garlic (1 bulb)
- Green peas (1 cup)
- Jicama (1)
- Kale (1 bunch)
- Kiwi (1)
- Lemons (4)
- Mango (2)
- Mixed berries (1 pint)
- Onion (3)

- Red bell peppers (3)
- Red onion (2)
- Romaine lettuce (1 head)
- Snap peas (1 cup)
- Spinach (2 bags)
- Sweet potatoes (4)
- Zucchini (5)

Pantry Staples

- Almond butter (1 jar)
- Almond milk, unsweetened (1 quart)
- Apple cider vinegar (1 bottle)
- Balsamic vinegar (1 bottle)
- Canned black beans (2 cans)
- Canned chickpeas (3 cans)
- Canned coconut milk, unsweetened (1 can)
- Chia seeds (1 bag)
- Chickpea flour (1 bag)
- Cocoa powder (1 container)
- Coconut aminos (1 bottle)
- Coconut oil (1 jar)
- Dried green lentils (1 bag)
- Dried red lentils (1 bag)
- Dried thyme (1 jar)
- Extra virgin olive oil (1 bottle)
- Flaxseed, ground (1 bag)
- Ground cinnamon (1 jar)
- Ground cumin (1 jar)
- Ground turmeric (1 jar)
- Honey (1 jar)
- Maple syrup (1 bottle)
- Nutmeg (1 jar)
- Oats (1 container)
- Pine nuts (1 small bag)
- Pumpkin seeds (1 bag)
- Quinoa (1 bag)
- Raisins (1 small bag)
- Rice vinegar (1 bottle)
- Sesame oil (1 bottle)
- Sesame seeds (1 small bag)
- Smoked paprika (1 jar)
- Soy sauce, gluten-free (1 bottle)
- Tahini (1 jar)
- Whole-grain bread (1 loaf)
- Whole-grain tortillas (1 package)
- Wild rice (1 bag)

Proteins

- Eggs (1 dozen)
- Goat cheese (1 package)
- Grilled chicken breasts (4)
- Ground turkey (1 pound)
- Salmon fillets (4)
- Shrimp, large (1 pound)
- Smoked salmon (1 package)
- Turkey breast slices (1 package)
- Cod fillets (2)

- Greek yogurt, plain (1 container)
- Sunflower seed butter (1 jar)

Herbs and Spices

- Basil leaves, fresh (1 bunch)
- Cayenne pepper (1 jar)
- Cinnamon (1 jar)
- Cumin (1 jar)
- Dill, fresh (1 bunch)
- Fresh parsley (1 bunch)
- Garlic powder (1 jar)
- Ground coriander (1 jar)
- Ground ginger (1 jar)
- Nutmeg (1 jar)
- Oregano (1 jar)
- Paprika (1 jar)
- Smoked paprika (1 jar)
- Thyme (1 jar)
- Turmeric (1 jar)

Made in the USA
Monee, IL
09 December 2024

73047837R00050